Financial Principles Simplified

A Comprehensive ⑦ **STEP** **Retirement Planning System**

L.I.F.E. Formula —
Live. Imagine. Focus. Enjoy.®

John F. Cicotte, CFP®, EA

LifePhase
Publishing

Financial Principles Simplified

Published in the United States of America by LifePhase Publishing 2017

10 9 8 7 6 5 4 3 2 1

Library of Congress Control Number: 2017913865
ISBN 13: 978-0-9993484-0-6

Cover formatted by: Kenneth W. Anderson

An acknowledgement of gratitude is extended to the National Institute of Retirement Security for permission to reprint the summary of "Retirement Security 2017: A Roadmap for Policy Makers: Americans' Views of the Retirement Crisis and Solutions," by Diane Oakley and Kelly Kenneally.

The purpose of this book is to help educate the reader. The author has researched many sources to ensure the most accurate and up-to-date information about this complex topic. Understandably, changes in government regulations, tax laws, and retirement planning principles and strategies may alter suggestions presented herein. Consequently, this book is sold with the understanding the publisher and author assume no liability or responsibility for any losses that may be suffered or alleged to be suffered, directly or indirectly, using the information presented in this book, and any liability is expressly disclaimed. The reader is encouraged to enlist professional advisers for all legal, tax, insurance, financial, and investment-related endeavors.

Published by: LifePhase Publishing

P.O. Box 2924
Granite Bay, CA 95746-9998
916-742-7722

Circular 230 Disclaimer: If and to the extent this book contains any tax advice, I am required by the Internal Revenue Service's Circular 230 (31 CFR Part 10) to advise you that such tax advice is not a formal legal opinion and is not intended or written to be used by you, and may not be used by you, (i) for the purpose of avoiding tax penalties that might be imposed on you or (ii) for promoting, marketing or recommending to another party any transaction or matter addressed herein.

John F. Cicotte, CFP®, EA is a registered principal with and securities offered through LPL Financial. Member FINRA/SIPC.

About the Author

John is married to Carol, his high school sweetheart. They have two surviving children, John and Jill, and one deceased child, Lisa. Their two grandchildren, Sarah and Christopher were the magnets that attracted them to the Sacramento, California area from the Sonoma County Wine Country in 2000. They took up residence in El Dorado Hills, California where they have lived for 17 years.

John loves being a husband, father, and papa. He is devoted to his wife, proud of his children, dotes on the grandchildren, and says, "Out of all the sons-in-law in the whole-wide world, Jill's husband, Tim, is my favorite."

It was way back in the year of our Lord, one thousand nine hundred eighty-seven that John received his certification as a CERTIFIED FINANCIAL PLANNER™ (CFP®) professional. He wanted to learn a comprehensive and skilled procedure of advising clients who needed to plan for retirement. He knew that tax implications were inherent in financial recommendations so two years later he obtained his designation from the U.S. Treasury Department as an Enrolled Agent.

John has a small retirement/financial planning practice in Roseville, California.

Acknowledgments

It has been more than 30 years since I helped my first clients plan their future. Subsequently, I have accumulated abundantly more wisdom than when I prepared that first plan. Thirty years of knowledge is a legacy I want to pass on to others. How can I? Write a book. Easier said than done, but with the help of family, clients, friends, and colleagues, this immense challenge evolved into an enthusiastic must-do mission, which took more than three years.

My wife, Carol, bless her heart, has been my writer's rock. Her patience, fearless common-sense input, intelligence and grandmother's kindness kept me focused. My son, John, and daughter, Jill, were my motivation to keep pushing forward.

Clients are people with big hearts. Those that I work for have the biggest hearts in the world, and they have taught me so much. I cannot thank them enough for their trust, support and loyalty. Trish Vichi and Paul Radcliffe offered positive suggestions about this book and were brave enough to remind me that poorly chosen words can inadvertently sound condescending.

When I told my friend Hollis McNatt about this project and that I needed a beta reader, he said, "I'll do it."

I said, "No. A beta reader is someone who doesn't know you. It's the only way to get an honest evaluation. Friends don't want to hurt your feelings."

He said, "You don't know me, do you?"

"Hollis, I'm so happy we had that conversation. You gave me the hard facts and pointed me in the right direction. I needed that. Thank you from the bottom of my heart."

I don't believe in Murphy's Law, but I do know I'm not perfect and mistakes can happen. To help correct any slipups or miscalculations I may have made in writing and rewriting this book, I asked six proven professionals for help in reviewing the manuscript.

John Campaigne, CFP® reviewed the manuscript with the skill of a seasoned professional and helped me perfect its contents.

My friends Patrick J. Orelli, CPA, and Justin M. Gilbert, attorney, provided their technical expertise. Pat reviewed all tax-related topics for clarity and accuracy. Justin tackled the chapter on estate planning and smoothed out the rough edges.

Joan said, "When two verbs (in this case "fuels" and "confuses") share a subject and the subject is not repeated, there should be no comma separating the two verb clauses. The only exception to this is if the reader might misinterpret."

Joan explained more writing rules to me than I will ever be able to remember. It was reassuring when I realized, I don't need to remember them with Joan by my side. Who is Joan? Joan D. Saunders, Saunders Editorial Services, a writer's guardian angel.

More angels, Mary Lou Anderson, author, came into my life late in the process. She helped refine the cover message and provided technical assistance. A special "thank you" to Shane-Lea Murphy, who helped with the compliance review.

When the thought of writing this book started tugging at my every waking hour, I wondered if I could finish such an undertaking. It did not take long to grasp the answer—I needed help. Everyone mentioned above contributed significantly to what you are about to learn.

To all, I extend my deep and sincere appreciation. Thank you to each of you for your professional support and friendship.

STOP! Read This First

THIS IS A STORY ABOUT PEOPLE like you, with the same hopes, dreams, and fears about the future. It will help you paint a picture of what you want your retirement to include.

One dictionary definition of "retire" is to withdraw from active life, from circulation; to go away to a place of privacy, shelter, or seclusion." Retirement is none of those things. Think of retire-ment as a time of "rebirth-ment." A new beginning. A new adventure. An exciting journey into the best life can offer. A time to reward yourself after years of hard work and self-sacrifice. It is life's dessert. Although different people enjoy different flavors, everyone's recipe has common ingredients. These pages can help channel your thoughts and actions so you can discover your recipe. They will help reveal what makes you feel joyful and fulfilled. You will explore whatever feels left undone and how to capture it, instead of letting it slip through your fingers. It is a way to plan your life after paychecks stop.

Plotting your future takes some planning. Perhaps you are retired, or close to retirement, and wondering, "What will the rest of my life look like?" Or maybe you are a take-charge younger person who knows it is never too early to find your recipe. "How do I overcome common obstacles and capture my dream?" you ask. My answer? Conquer everyone's first planning problem—complexity. It is the enemy of execution. Complexity fuels procrastination and confuses your good intentions. Choosing the path of least resistance, doing nothing, leads to failure. Do not let the thorny uncertainties ahead stop you from reaching for your rose.

Visualize happiness and manage your money to help support your vision.

This book will help guide you to your idea of a happier life.

It is neither a panacea nor a guarantee of an implied outcome. Nothing in these pages should be construed as promissory. Instead, you can use this story to help inspire you to study the unknown so you can learn how to navigate this exciting chapter of your life, whether it is around the corner or years in the future. It will encourage you with powerful ideas, concepts, and motivation. You will learn how to nourish your aspirations so you can grow them into a relaxed and pleasurable lifestyle. Your results will depend on your choices and on the specific action steps you complete. Your future happiness depends on you, no one else, and your implementation of the action steps you are about to learn.

No one wants a book that is full of unfamiliar financial and investment vernacular, so, as much as possible, you will see the use of technical terms and financial jargon minimized and a bold attempt to simplify problematic material. However, be on notice that the true scope of retirement planning is complicated.

Most chapters consist of two parts: The Story and The Nitty-Gritty. The Story exposes critical planning issues that you need to be aware of and, when necessary, fix. The Nitty-Gritty sections help you wrap your brain around the complexities that come up in The Story sections. You picked up this book because you want to learn how you can have a better future, and that is what will happen as you absorb the concepts, principles, and action steps discussed in The Nitty-Gritty sections. This dual approach means an engaging reading experience, which will stimulate the receptive regions of your brain with techniques that will invigorate your intellectual juices. You will be rewarded when you exploit these noteworthy tactics. Learning new and exciting ways to add money to your retirement bankroll will be fun.

My purpose in writing this book? "To give you basic tools to help you pursue your financial and retirement goals." You can achieve your "rebirth-ment" dream. Immerse yourself in these pages. Internalize the lessons. Implement each action step. Strive to achieve your ambitions. Believe that with knowledge, positive expectations, and follow-through comes the ability to make it happen!

The process of creating a secure and comfortable life will be an exciting, albeit rocky journey. What you are about to undertake will require some effort; but it is work that you must do. Think of it as an endeavor that may produce immense pleasure and happiness.

You will take control by learning to:

1. Recognize which factors will increase your financial happiness;

2. Partition your economic life into understandable segments;

3. Satisfy your needs as well as whoop it up and enjoy your wants; and

4. Pinpoint a dedicated, well-qualified retirement planning professional, a trained expert who knows how to guide you along the pathway—a CFP®.* She will help simplify and clarify your financial life and will try to make the planning process as trouble-free as possible. She will need your participation—and when you finish this book, you will have the knowledge required to do your part.

Through The Story section of each chapter, you will come to know your new friends, Lisa and Mark Dolan. They are confused and worried about the prospect of retirement coming in nine years. Amazingly, a mystical CFP®, Ace Sorts, visits Mark in his dreams to teach and inspire him with planning instructions. You will witness each rich, intense, and lucid tutorial. As you read, ask yourself, could Ace Sorts be a real person who has the power to connect with Mark through his dreams?

You will also get to know Chico Jetton, CFP®, founder and owner of Chico Jetton Retirement, Inc. Your first introduction to Chico will be in a Nitty-Gritty section—he has helped a do-it-yourself investor who realized he did not know everything he needed to know about life planning. Later, Chico will introduce you to his seven-step L.I.F.E. Formula—Live. Imagine. Focus. Enjoy.® A comprehensive 7-step retirement planning system.

All this information will enable you to prepare to experience your most thrilling journey: life after work.

This is a BIG deal. DREAM BIG! SAVE BIG! LIVE BIG!

*Some financial advisers have other credentials, and they may have the years of experience, training, and knowledge necessary to help you, especially those whose business model embraces what this book teaches.

He who knows not and knows not that he knows not,
He is a fool—shun him;
He who knows not and knows he knows not,
He is simple—teach him;
He who knows and knows not he knows,
He is asleep—wake him;
He who knows and knows he knows,
He is wise—follow him.
—Author Unknown

Nosce te ipsum.
—Latin

Know thyself.
—English

Employ your time in improving
yourself by other men's writings,
so that you shall gain easily
what others have labored hard for.
—Socrates

Contents

1

MECHANICS OF PLANNING

Two Possible Methods

The Story

THE MORNING SQUEEZED PAST THE edges of the window shades, creating a sliver of light. Mark Dolan awoke from his fascinating, but troubling dream. His journey through the night, filled with twists, turns, anxiety, fear, excitement, and hope, had fashioned the covers into makeshift handcuffs. He attempted to liberate his right arm, tangled and buried under the covers. Once freed, he rubbed his eyes until he could focus on the day and then realized it was Saturday. He sat up and grabbed his robe.

"Honey, we have to do it. We just have to do it," he

said to Lisa, his wife of 33 years, as she slid into warm slippers.

"Good morning," Lisa said. "Yep, you're right. We can't stay in bed all day."

"No, no, that's not what I mean."

"Well?"

"You know these dreams I've been having? They're telling me ways to plan our retirement."

"You had another one?" she asked with a sideways glance.

Mark followed Lisa into the bathroom.

"Pass the toothpaste, please," he said. "Yeah, I was learning the details of the final lesson—"

"What final lesson?"

He looked into the mirror at Lisa's reflection. He searched his mind to retrieve convincing words.

I need her help and her perspective, he thought. *She's so strong, despite or perhaps because of her difficult childhood. Six younger siblings, an alcoholic father, a chronically ill mother whose care fell mostly on her shoulders. I can't imagine having to be the "mother" at such an early age, doing all the cleaning, shopping, cooking. She never got to enjoy a normal childhood, yet somehow she managed to graduate from college, and with honors. It's a miracle she still wanted to have kids!*

And the kids and I are lucky, the beneficiaries of her well-honed life skills, which I sure need now.

"Each of these dreams makes me realize that we don't have a retirement plan. I'm worried. This person in my dreams is teaching me things that have never crossed my mind. I'm learning concepts that our broker hasn't talked about.

"He has an odd name, too—Ace. Ace Sorts."

"You're kidding. A first and a last name for a guy you're dreaming about?" She made no attempt to hide her surprise or the chuckle that accompanied it.

"We should pay attention to his teachings," Mark insisted. "My sense is that I'm learning true wisdom." Lisa raised an eyebrow.

He ignored her apparent skepticism. "Anyway, he refers to his set of seven lessons as *The Retirement Dream Solution*. It's a way to help us plan our happiness, to help us avoid financial glitches and blunders along the way. He said that I need to get my financial and retirement ducks in a row. He uses that duck line a lot. He calls them dollar ducks. Part of what he talks about includes rules on intelligent investing, but he told me that investing is only one component of a much bigger picture. Last night he started to explain a crucial lesson—number seven. He began giving me the details, but I woke up before he could finish.

"The dreams are urging me to do something. They're fascinating and stimulating, and they feel real. I have mixed emotions. I like them, but at the same time, they churn up feelings of dread . . . maybe about the unknown. I've been telling you about them—have you been listening?"

Lisa put her towel down and stretched, still trying to wake up. "Yep, you have; sorry, I guess I've only been half-listening. Forgive me? I'm going downstairs, gonna make some coffee. Do you want French press or regular drip?"

"French press. Then we need to finish this conversation."

"Okay, count on it. But over coffee please!" She smiled at him, collected dirty clothes from the hamper, and went down to the kitchen.

After 33 years of marriage, she knew her man well. He had an air of confidence that everyone admired and envied. *Oh, brother, he's not going to let up—he never does,* she thought. *A small price to pay, I guess, when someone's so loving, always upbeat and forever smiling.*

I'm so fortunate. All our years together, his love and devotion haven't wavered. And John and Jill only made our bond stronger. Their relationship with him—wow, so different from mine with my father. Even now, John, at 30, and Jill, at 29, rely on their dad to help them see which factors to consider before they make life decisions, but without telling them what to do. I loved our family meetings when we'd talk about the kids and the family's issues: school, vacation destinations, girls, boys, current events. I can picture John and Angela having the same talks with Sarah and Christopher when they get a little older. And Jill and Tim, it's so exciting they're expecting their first child after being married four years. And I'm sure they'll do the same thing. How to communicate is not a bad legacy to pass on. She smiled to herself. *Yep, Mark and I did a darn good job with our parenting.*

As Lisa worked her way around the kitchen, she could not help thinking about what Mark had said. *Sure, the message seems to ring true, but . . . in a dream?* Retirement had always been a subject hidden in the back of her mind. Was this a good time to change gears, put it at the forefront?

How do I plan something when I have no knowledge of what must be done? Do I wing it? Do I learn from a book? How do I pick the right book? Do I ask my friends? Would they know? She sighed. *If only life were simpler.*

She had better press the coffee, focus on that—much less complicated.

She started to grind the beans into breadcrumb-sized chunks, enough to make eight cups. She watched as the aromatic pills ricocheted back and forth, circling inside the grinder like the questions that troubled her. Next, she turned on the instant hot water tap and covered the energizing fragments with 205-degree filtered water. After one minute, she stirred the bloom. After three more, she would press their morning elixir.

Lisa sat and waited, propping her elbows on the table, cradling her face, looking out the window as the day continued to dawn. She wanted to neutralize her confusion and uncertainty and have a private moment of reflection. *Should I finish that conversation? The subject must be addressed, but Mark's dreams . . . are they really a sign? Am I ready to complicate my life more? Is now a good time?*

Stop! Stop! Stop! Her inner struggle was spoiling what had always been a pleasure—watching the morning sun crest the horizon.

Finally, the secondhand had circled past the 12 three times. Press the beans. Done. She sat with her cup, returning to her reflections. *Could this be a problem or might it be an opportunity disguised?* She knew the answer. She knew what she—they—must do. They must begin.

The Nitty-Gritty

So when you have decided it is time for a retirement plan, where do you start? How do you get ready?

There are two common approaches to creating a plan for retirement: cash flow–based and goals–based. Either can be used to build a roadmap to travel through time. The cash flow format is replete with assumptions leading up to your retirement date. You will need to track your income, taxes, living expenses, and discretionary spending for all years. It is necessary to recalculate your assumptions every year in order to maintain accuracy. In other words, tons of numbers.

The goals-based technique focuses less on data. This approach does not require constant tracking of all your expenses. You only need to know how much you are saving for retirement, the total value of your retirement assets, and if any pre-retirement expenses will be paid from those funds. When such expenses are paid from income, then no additional accounting is necessary. With the goals-based technique, you do not need to list expenses or make a variety of assumptions that must be revised each year.

There is one exception: If your analysis reveals you are not saving enough money to achieve your goals, you will need to increase savings. The only way you can effectively do that is to list all your expenses and then identify the expenses that can be converted to savings.

Using the goals-based approach is easier. But as you get closer to your retirement date, it makes sense to know your annual household operating outlay. Add to that number your discretionary outflows to get accurate totals. You should know your number, not just a number that is in the ballpark.

You might think that this number would be easy to come up with. It is not. It requires research. If you have been keeping track of your income and expenses using bookkeeping software, the process is easier. But whether you have been recording your information by hand or by computer, you must examine your checkbook register, credit card statements, and miscellaneous spending to find your number. Add income tax payments, savings, contributions to retirement plans, gifts, charitable donations, and other expenses to your list. When finished, you should be able to identify 95 percent of your living and discretionary expenses. Anything less means you must keep searching because this number is the foundation from which you project all your future income needs and wants.

When you have your number, subtract what will no longer be necessary when you retire, for example, employment fees, union dues, license fees, educational expenses, work clothing, and so on. You will no longer be driving to and from work, which may translate into lower premiums on auto insurance. Put your thinking cap on—you will be surprised by what you discover.

Also consider new purchases that you will need to make. Sure, it is difficult to project, but try. Judge when you might buy a new car, reroof your home, and take vacations—maybe that dream vacation. You will need to think of other demands, possibly education expenses for you, your children, and grandchildren, extraordinary medical expenses, short-term dreams, special gifts, perhaps golf lessons and mini trips. Take into account whether you might need to provide care for a parent, a child with special needs, or a spouse. Each family situation looks different. Work at it, and you will be surprised with what you will see. If you have a CFP®, she will make this part of the planning process much easier. If you do not have a CFP® yet, this might be the time to establish a relationship with one. (See Chapter 7 for help in learning how to find and what to look for in a CFP®.)

When you are working with these numbers, beware! You have an enemy looting your financial goals—inflation. The only way you can defeat your foe is to know it well. When you think about inflation, you probably think about paying more for a loaf of bread. You are right about that. However, when it comes to your retirement goals, you must look at inflation from another perspective. To understand the enemy, think of it as the loss of purchasing power.

Imagine that the odds are in your favor and you will live another 30 years after you retire. Assume the purchasing power of a $100 bill today is worth $100, that is, your $100 bill will buy $100 worth of goods and services. If the inflation rate over the next 30 years increases at only 2 percent, that same $100 bill is still $100, but it will buy only $54.55 of goods and services.

Of course, inflation over the next 30 years could average more than 2 percent. If you are an older baby boomer, you remember the Great Inflation decade, the 1970s. If you are a younger baby boomer, you were a young teenager, but you still may remember that the cost of a night at the movies went way up, taking a bigger bite out of your allowance or the money you earned at a part-time job.

According to U.S. Bureau of Labor Statistics, the inflation rate in 1974, was 8.3 percent, and it topped out at 12.4 percent in 1980.

Know your enemy. Keep your eyes peeled. Your enemy is there, watching you every day, even after you quit working. It is peeking through your window at night, following you when you go to the coffee shop, showing up everywhere you go. It is there looking over your shoulder when you are on vacation. Although quiet, unassuming, and invisible to the naked eye, it strangles your purchasing power without mercy. You need to defend yourself. You retire, but inflation does not. It may take some time off occasionally, but it never quits. It is there, lurking in the darkness, and it is after your money.

When your CFP® performs your reviews, the actual inflation rate will be compared with your projected rate to see if it is accurate. What? Your CFP® performs reviews? Yes! You must review your plan regularly. Remember what you read earlier. Your "rebirth-ment" is an exciting new adventure, a new beginning—but it is not a destination. It is a thrilling journey that comprises the best that life can offer. You are traveling a toll road, and you must keep paying the tolls. They will include roadblocks, detours, and adjustments along the way. At some point, you may decide to go a different direction. You and your CFP® must recalibrate your route each year in order to make sure you stay on the road to living the good life.

If the initial forecasts suggest you might run out of money before you leave this Earth, you must adjust something. Save more money. Invest wisely. Change your spending patterns, work longer, work part-time, or scale down your monthly outlays. Maybe move to a state that has lower income taxes or no taxes. According to the Tax Foundation, there are seven states that do not have an income tax, and two that tax only dividends and interest.

It is complicated.

2

CHECK YOUR DNA

Your Other DNA

The Story

SUDDENLY, A LOUD VOICE BROKE Lisa's trance-like solitude.

"I'm hungry. Tell me what to do to help."

Startled, she looked up to see Mark's 5'11", 175-pound frame filling the doorway. She admired his black hair, with its sophisticated sprinkling of silver. His dark eyes were revealing more than his confident, George Clooney smile.

"Sorry," he said. "What are you thinking about?"

"Come on, you know."

"My dreams?"

"No. Well, yes. I'm thinking about what your dreams are teaching you: that we need to plan your retirement, *our* retirement." She paused, then said, a little uncertainly, "But we don't know how."

Mark smiled, glad to finally have her undivided attention. "Okay, I hear you loud and clear," he said. "I feel the way you do. But we can talk about it, can't we?"

"Yep, of course. We *should*."

"I agree. My dreams woke me up—figuratively, that is," he grinned. Then he got serious. "We can't keep putting off dealing with our future. If we wait, it could be too late. Does that make sense?"

"Of course. You've been giving me bits and pieces about what you've learned from the lessons. So now, tell me more. Explain why the last lesson's so crucial." She stood up to get the coffee.

"Ace said the first six lessons won't work without number seven."

"Well, how are you going to learn the final one if you keep waking up before he explains it?"

"I don't know. He must repeat the lessons."

Mark sat on his customary chair and looked around the room. His eyes stopped, fixing on Lisa as she poured coffee. She looked taller than 5'6", and her hair color and blue eyes brought to mind a young Goldie Hawn.

He appreciated everything about her. She provided the motivation he needed to follow through on projects she considered important. He needed her to take ownership of this endeavor, otherwise, he feared, it might not get done.

Hopefully, Lisa asked, "Well, we do have a plan, don't we? We can get better organized, but do we need to do something other than that? I like the idea of, well, continuing our normal routine. I mean, we're planning everything right, aren't we? Tell me we are."

Mark had a ready answer, but should he put her at ease or tell her the truth? *I'm not going to avoid this and let her think everything is okay. Ace has made it apparent to me that we don't have anything that resembles a real plan. Our intention, to not run out of money before we both die, is not what a person with average intelligence would call a plan. It's just a hope, without any connection to a comprehensive strategy.*

"Honey, I hate to say it, but we don't have a plan."

He waited for her reaction, but there was only silence. Clearly, she wanted him to continue. So he did.

"In one of my earlier dreams, Ace had an interesting—and I might say profound—way to demonstrate the importance of having a plan. He said that on July 16, 1969, when NASA put Neal Armstrong into the *Apollo* spacecraft, they told him that they had a well-thought-out way to get him safely to the moon. Armstrong responded by asking if they had a well-thought-out plan to get him safely home."

Lisa looked at her husband. She knew he wanted her on board. Did she fear the unknown? Something in the back of her mind, an internal voice, or perhaps a survival mechanism, urged her to forge ahead.

"I hear you, Mark. But I'm not sure how to go about figuring this out, and it's making me anxious. I'm concerned that there's more to it than we know. I realize we're not talking about putting a man on the moon, but we are talking about planning the rest of our lives. I mean, my gut confirms that we should be doing more. And it's obvious you're passionate about these dreams. But—"

"Yeah, Ace says intriguing things. Last night he told me that we need to know our DNA."

"Our DNA? Why on Earth? Are you going to tell me we have to get a blood test or saliva swab?"

Mark laughed. "No. Not the genetic information; it has to do with traits and features that characterize our human uniqueness. Ace said it relates to the depth and scope of our personal feelings about life, its gravity, and the complexities that make up who we are at our roots.

"He said another thing that got my attention."

"What?"

"He told me about a Census Bureau statistic that reported something scary."

"Come on, Mark."

"No, listen. He informed me that the Census Bureau found that 51 percent of women over the age of 69 are widowed. I don't plan on dying that early, but we need to make sure that you have adequate resources, including sufficient income, and that our ducks are in a row if I do check out ahead of schedule. If that happens, you get my Social Security, but you lose yours. Ace also said your income tax situation will get worse because you would have to file as a single person, which could increase your taxes. He gave me some other negative examples, but they were a little vague."

"You're not going to die early!" Her voice was tinged with apprehension, and then she said, "Let's get back to the lessons he talked about."

"Yeah, okay," Mark said, happy she was asking questions. "Ace said that investing money intelligently is vital, but emphasized that there's more to a successful retirement than just investing money. There's more to it than people know or think about. That's why he developed the seven lessons in *The Retirement Dream*

Solution."

"It sounds like you've learned a lot from him. What should we do to get started?"

"I like your attitude, honey. Ace said that there are two types of people: those who make things happen, Group 1; and those who just let things happen, Group 2. Hearing you ask questions is music to my ears, and it's a Group 1 trait."

Lisa said, "The concept of the two groups sounds interesting. But what's the first lesson about? Can you give me more details?"

"The first lesson makes us imagine what we want our life to include when we retire."

The Nitty-Gritty

In our story, Ace alerted Mark to the tax and social security problems that Lisa would face if he died. It is something folks rarely think about, much less talk about.

Death of a spouse has a negative impact on the surviving spouse's income tax status if that person does not remarry. The survivor would have to file as a single filer unless a dependent child lived in the home, which would allow filing as a widow(er) for two years. In this case, the tax rate would be the same, but there would be a loss of the deceased person's personal exemption, and the filing status would change after two years to a single filer. Taxes could be more expensive because of the change of filing status and the loss of the personal exemption.

When it comes to social security, if both people were receiving benefits, the larger of the two would be continued, but the lower amount would be lost.

When preparing for future possibilities, people have one of two attitudes about controlling their life. Group 1 sees the positives that will support achievement of success. Group 2 sees the negatives that might cause failure. A massive gap separates these two mindsets. Group 1 personalities have clear, action-based expectations. They have confidence that their abilities and smart choices will make things go their way. Group 2 personalities let the chips fall where they may, hoping things turn out well, seldom trying to control their outcome. They may even blame outside forces for their life's predicaments. Fortunately, they are not stuck there. They can cross the abyss on wings of optimism to reach the other side.

You must control life, or life will control you.

If you have clear-cut, action-rooted expectations, then you are already aware that you benefit from following the guidance of experts. If you dwell on the negative side of things, then I hope you come to realize that seeking the help of a CFP® will strengthen seemingly external circumstances in your favor!

Are you in Group 1 or 2? If your answer is that it does not matter, then you are in Group 2 and your chips will fall. Nevertheless, hope reigns supreme. Taking precise action will feed the adrenalin you need in order to adjust your perspective, to solidify hope. Engagement, decisiveness, and change of habit will build a bridge from your Group 2 nature to the other side. Becoming aware of the advantage of being "teachable" will motivate you to start planning and will lead you toward success.

Taking the time necessary to plan an event is easy—if it is a week or two in the future. Taking the time needed to plan an event five years or more in the future is easy, too—easy to put off.

What is time? Time is invisible. You cannot see it, you cannot touch, smell, taste, or hear it. Time is mysterious. Is it real? Is it your friend or enemy? Does time control you or do you control time? Do you have a choice? Time is more than days, weeks, months, and years. It is your companion and treasure.

Time is life! And life is finite. A day lost to the clock cannot be recovered. Start your journey toward fulfillment today, and I will hold your hand and walk with you.

Ben Franklin said, "By failing to prepare, you are preparing to fail."

Will preparation help you predict what your future holds? No. Can you predict the *probable* future? Yes. How? Follow these steps.

First, adopt the traits of a Group I person: become open, be willing to seek and implement proven strategies that can influence a positive outcome.

Second, plan and organize. Or, as Ben Franklin's message proclaimed, prepare. You are doing that by reading this book.

And third, take action. Do it.

Now let the "fun" continue! Jumping into the world of controlling your future makes sense, but is not easy. It takes effort. However, when following a financial guide, *you* can become a Group I member. Your knowledge and confidence will grow. You will feel more powerful and more able to survive the inevitable mishaps along the way.

It is time to start Lesson One. Get paper and pencil. Start

writing. You will have fun. It will help you see a vision of life after you retire. Use your imagination to get deeply introspective. Visualize your needs, desires, expectations, concerns, and goals. To begin, paint a picture in your mind, then imagine being in that picture. Let yourself go to that place. See it. Feel it.

The colors of life are varied: different hues, tints, dyes, and shades. Your brushstrokes will reveal your wants, wishes, and possibilities. This lesson inspires a method of self-examination, a way to look within to discover your DNA, which in this instance means—"dimensional natural attitudes." They are the nongenetic virtues that define your individuality: the talents, thoughts, attributes, behaviors, feelings about your intrinsic worth, and inner spark that manifest who you are. All those traits determine your choice of pleasures. They provoke your desires and involvement. It is a way to explore your deepest feelings about what will make your life more rewarding, to pinpoint social and environmental conditions that can help promote long-lasting happiness, passion, and pleasure. Ultimately, it is a way to come to the realization that you can enjoy life's abundance!

Your life will change dramatically. Get prepared. Do you want to continue your current lifestyle? If you do, then decide which activities will replace the time that your work occupied. What are your concerns? Must you or will you make a big change, like selling your home so you can downsize or move closer to grandchildren? Maybe you want to move to a state that has a lower tax system and use your savings to travel or to survive.

A move, regardless of the reason, can be major and should

be considered with extreme caution, particularly if you are moving to a different state. Take the time necessary to make a smart choice. Rent before you buy.

Have you identified special pleasures you would like to experience before you kick the bucket? When you put your plan in motion, you may be able to check off some of the items on your bucket list before you retire.

One of these might be to go back to school to learn a new language, a musical instrument, or a time-tested secret desire. Do your deepest feelings draw you to helping others? There are rock-solid, worthwhile organizations that cannot survive without dedicated volunteers. The world needs you.

Take some time, think about the experiences that have made you happy, then make them part of your vision. Consider this your opportunity to do things you have been putting off.

Your secret desire may be to change careers to pursue your passion. Something that would be fun to do, not work. Perhaps you have thought about starting your own business. This would be the time to act, to evaluate what is needed to make it plausible. Do your homework and make it happen.

If a layoff, health issues, age, or other circumstances forced retirement upon you, adjust your actions to reduce stress. Take the steps necessary to make your financial life easier to manage.

Above all, the life you seek is composed of happiness, passion, and pleasure. As you paint the picture of what you want, your brushstrokes will reveal your aspirations and opportunities, and you will feel an edge-of-the-chair anticipation. All the colorful, exciting puzzle pieces of life are exposed, then joined together to create a masterpiece—your masterpiece.

Act now. What do you see? Put your dream on paper. Complete Lesson One. It is not complicated.

3

FIDUCIARY OR NONFIDUCIARY

What You Need to Know

The Story

"HONEY, DO YOU REMEMBER WHEN Pat and Phil brought us those delicious venison steaks a few weeks ago?" Mark asked. "Of course, I do. It was February. Three months ago."

"That long? Well, that's when I had my first dream. And they're so real—each one makes me feel as though I'm at the movie theater. It's like they're in high-definition color with 7.1-channel digital wraparound sound. Ace has taught me stuff I've never thought about and shown me interesting concepts our brokers have never mentioned. And it all makes sense to me. Sure, we've had investment brokers tell us how to invest our money, but they all talk 'investment talk.' Words *they* understand. Sometimes I think I'm doing better with the accounts I manage than what Evelyn is doing for us. Remember the last time we went to meet with her?

"Sure, I remember. What about it?"

"She's a stockbroker, a salesperson. Her job is to sell investment products, not to help us plan our future. In one dream—I remember this part vividly—Ace presented what I would call an exposé. He told me the difference between a fiduciary and a nonfiduciary. Honey, we should have someone helping us who is acting as a fiduciary."

"I know what 'fiduciary' means," she said. "But how does it relate to investments?"

"It means we have to pay attention. Ace said a fiduciary is like an advocate, someone who helps us. A fiduciary must make recommendations that are in our best interests, not that give them the highest commissions and fees."

She seemed a bit skeptical. "Don't all people who sell investments have to do that?"

"No. It's complicated. Ace said the Department of Labor, and then he called it the DOL, has introduced a new regulation that would require brokers to act as fiduciaries when managing retirement accounts, but not after-tax accounts. That may come later when the Securities and Exchange Commission gets around to it. The DOL only has regulatory control over retirement accounts.

"Ace said brokers selling regular investments are just salespeople, and they're only required to sell what's termed a 'suitable investment.'"

Lisa looked confused. "Well, that sounds like the same thing to me."

"Yeah, it did to me, too. But there's a difference. Ace told me that some investments could qualify as being suitable, but be a bad choice because of the kind of investment it is and its commissions and fees. When a fiduciary sells an investment, it must not only be suitable, but also have low fees and no commissions."

"This sounds more involved than I thought it would be."

"Me, too. But then I was thinking about this at work, and something dawned on me—and I'm a little embarrassed that I'd never thought of it before."

"What?" Lisa asked.

"Well, when we moved into this home, we hired an interior decorator and a landscape architect. When we have electrical problems, we hire an electrician. I hired a cardiologist to get my blood pressure under control. We hired Dr. Reynolds to keep tabs on our eyes. You hired a specialist to fix your feet—"

"Okay, so, my feet are doing fine. Get to your point."

"It's as plain as the toes on your feet." He laughed at his little joke, then said, "When we need help with something important, we hire a specialist."

"Well, okay—and?"

"Honey, consider this; we have the cars serviced on a regular basis, but we've never had a retirement specialist look at what might happen to us when we retire. Would you classify our retirement as important or insignificant?"

"Oh. Point made."

Mark's eyes opened wide to emphasize his point. "Dummy us! Why haven't we hired a pro to help us plan our retirement and invest our money? We need to get a CFP®. It's a repeated command from Ace."

"We're not dummies. It's, well, it's just something neither of us realized we should do. You've been handling a lot of it, and we both know how smart you are!" she said, grinning at him. "And also, we assumed Evelyn was keeping an eye on things. But it's true, when you give it a little thought, it's easy to see that we shouldn't count on her to do what she hasn't been educated to do. Remember what they say about making assumptions . . ."

"Yeah, I do." His eyebrows went up, and he rolled his eyes. He paused, then said, "You know, I learned something else that we need to talk about."

"There's more?" Lisa said. "This sounds ominous. I had better make breakfast. What would you like?"

Mark responded automatically. It was his favorite answer, especially on a Saturday or Sunday morning. "If I had some ham, I'd have some ham and eggs, if I had some eggs."

Lisa laughed. "I should've guessed. Okay, keep talking. What are you about to tell me that's so ominous?"

The Nitty-Gritty

Anyone who sells stocks, bonds, and related investments is required to be registered and must be affiliated with a broker/dealer.

The broker/dealer supervises the registered representative's operation and makes certain the representative works within regulatory guidelines. Annual audits are conducted to randomly review client files. The firm's advertising, emails, and other correspondence are also subject to regulatory monitoring.

The Bernie Madoff catastrophe occurred because Madoff played both roles, the registered representative and the broker/dealer. Gigantic mistake. The wolf guarding the hen house. The resulting mega disaster that crushed his investors could have been avoided if they would have followed this simple rule: keep the two entities separate. As the late president Ronald Reagan said, "Trust, but verify."

Equally as vital is that you know what a fiduciary is. This remains one of the best-kept secrets on Wall Street, but it is coming out of the closet. Unfortunately, finding out about it may shock, disappoint, and upset you. But do not despair—help is here.

When people want to invest their money, they have two primary resources. The first is an investment adviser. The second is an investment broker. Reread the two titles. You need to know that there is a difference. Most investors have not been told this important fact. You would think the advice from each would be the same. However, there is a significant disparity that focuses on loyalty. The investment adviser's required loyalty is to you, the investor. The investment broker's loyalty is to the broker/dealer.

The Investment Advisers Act of 1940 (the Act) regulates how investors must be treated. The U.S. Securities and Exchange Commission (SEC) and state security regulators are the watchdogs. The Act requires that an investment adviser act as a fiduciary while receiving a fee when advising you.

The Act does not regulate investment brokers. An investment broker is required only to sell a "suitable investment." An investment could qualify as suitable as it relates to your risk tolerance, asset category, allocation percentage to your other investments, and so on and still not be a good asset to own. It could be a bad investment with commissions and high fees.

When salespeople expect a commission, do they recommend what is best or do they push the investment that results in a big payday? Money motivates. Of course, there are properly inspired salespeople who would make a fitting recommendation. But are you able to see which is which?

There are sharp legal distinctions between the titles *investment adviser representative, investment broker, financial planner, financial adviser,* and *insurance agent.* Be alert to the differences. And be aware that the Act only regulates investment adviser representatives.

Fortunately, help is on the way. Transparency? Maybe. The Department of Labor believes salespeople have not treated investors fairly. Therefore, on April 6, 2016, it instituted a 1,023-page-long regulation requiring salespeople to act as fiduciaries when managing "qualified retirement accounts," like a 401(k) and IRA plans, a surprising result after facing stiff opposition from Wall Street. The regulation has been instituted on a trial basis, giving the industry time to adjust.

You will be a winner regardless of the final rule structure and effective date.

But until the SEC acts, you must decide which relationship you want when investing your "after-tax money." If you know which investment product you want and intend to keep it, then going to a salesperson and paying a commission might be a good option.

If you are planning your retirement dream, you may decide it is best to hire an independent CFP® who specializes in retirement planning and acts on your behalf as a fiduciary.

An investment adviser representative will charge you a fee, and this relationship eliminates the inherent conflict of interest with commission transactions.

Be on guard though. An investment adviser representative may wear two hats. She may act as an investment broker (salesperson) on your nonretirement accounts. You must know whether the person you are hiring is acting as a fee-based fiduciary under the definition of the Act, acting as a fee-based fiduciary under the new rule, or acting as a salesperson.

A CFP® can be both a fiduciary and a salesperson. Understand and know the difference. Question each transaction and learn whether you are paying a commission, a fee, or both. Buyer beware—it is your money.

Forewarned is forearmed. It is complicated.

4

NO ESTATE PLAN IS A SAD STATE

Nine Steps to Follow

The Story

"WELL, MARK, I'M WAITING. WHAT are you about to tell me that's so ominous?"

"Your word, not mine," he said. "I've learned that it's essential you attend our meetings with the retirement specialist we hire. We must be involved together so we can learn which action steps we should take to get our plan in writing; then we have to continue to work together to monitor our progress."

Lisa said, "But Evelyn told us that I didn't need to go to all the meetings if we discuss what you talked about." Her voice had an edge to it.

"I know what she told us, but my dreams have taught me that's a mistake. We need to attend the meetings together.

"Ace said that couples are a team, and everyone on the team must know the game plan. If one of us gets sick or dies, the other person needs to understand what to do and how to do it."

He could tell he had her full attention now, which was a good sign.

"Honey, his main point was the depth of hopelessness that consumes a person when a spouse dies. The enormous despair prevents the survivor from functioning with a balanced, emotional, and intellectual mindset. It's such a paralyzing experience, losing a spouse and also being faced with having to deal with finances, particularly if the survivor never participated in the process."

"He gave me two examples. He called it 'the power of two.' Would you like me to continue?"

"I suppose."

"The first story was about one of his golf buddies. His wife suffered a sudden, massive heart attack and died the next day, three weeks before their 39th wedding anniversary celebration. She was only 66. A devastating event. Instantly, this man's life became an emotional nightmare.

"Ace described his friend as an intelligent man, with an executive position at a major utility company. Even though he was a successful businessman, his wife's death paralyzed him. She was the one who had handled the finances. He knew how to write checks, but had no idea how to go about paying the bills, let alone any knowledge about their investment portfolio or how to adapt in four years to their planned retirement. He didn't even know her username or passwords on their accounts."

Lisa frowned. "Well, that's depressing."

"Yeah, a mess. Making a bad situation even worse, it left him unwilling to do anything with their investments because he was confused and unfamiliar with them. He said, 'That was what she did' and 'I don't want to go there.' He'd never been involved. Consequently, when she died, he had no idea what to do. He was in uncharted waters without a compass."

Mark continued, "Talking about death reminds me of something else important that we have been subconsciously ignoring."

"What, pray tell?"

"You're funny. How long has it been since we looked at our will and living trust? Any idea?"

"Hmm. I know where we keep it, I think, but that's it."

The Nitty-Gritty

To contemplate your death or the death of those you love is difficult; however, it is a necessary and important duty. Consider it an essential step that you must carry out if you want all your dollar ducks in a row. Living up to your responsibility will be a prideful moment.

When you die, the assets titled in your name need to be retitled in the name of a living person or an entity. The legal process used to end your legal affairs and transfer your property to your beneficiaries is called "probate." If you die without a will or living trust, the state where you reside will decide who receives your property and when. However, it may not distribute your property according to your wishes. The legal procedure is based on the laws of intestacy or intestate succession, which is why dying without a will is called "dying intestate." The rules are found in your state's Probate Code.

The phrase *estate planning* may conjure up thoughts in your mind of "not something I want to talk about" or "it's too complicated." Or you might say, "I don't have enough money. I don't need a will." You might be right, but perhaps not. Consider this. Your death could result from a negligent act by another person or corporation. If there were a lawsuit or settlement, those funds would be subject to the laws of intestacy. A will solves that problem.

To help you with this daunting, easy-to-ignore personal obligation, I am going to try to untangle this subject as much as possible. What I am about to explain is specific to California.

Your state may have different rules.

Instead of using the intestate succession provisions of the Probate Code to distribute your assets, you should have a qualified estate-planning attorney create a legal document. The best way to do this is to have your trust attorney make a will or a blend of a will and a living trust. Do not use an online program for something this important. Too much could go wrong, and there are no do-overs.

Note: When you use a living trust to distribute your assets, you still need a will. It is called a "pour-over will." Its primary purpose is to void your current will, nominate guardians for minor children, and pour-over (transfer) non-trust assets to your living trust after your death. However, you should *not* use the pour-over provision as a mechanism to fund (transfer assets to) your living trust at your death. Those assets will still go through probate before being transferred to the trust and, ultimately, distributed to your beneficiaries. Ask your estate-planning attorney to explain the mechanics of the pour-over will and why it is essential to title your property in the name of your trust before you die.

The choice between a stand-alone will and a living trust usually depends on the dollar value of all your assets and whether you own real estate.

If the gross value of your assets subject to probate (some assets are not subject to probate—see below) does not total more than $150,000 (including real estate) when you die, your assets may be distributed to your beneficiaries without a formal probate. This can be done through California's Independent Administration of Estates Act, which authorizes Small Estate Affidavits for financial accounts. However, for real property acquired during marriage with the earnings of one or both spouses, a surviving spouse can file a Spousal Property Petition. For non-spouse beneficiaries, the real property must first be appraised by a court-appointed appraiser, known as a probate referee. Also, persons entitled to the property must file a Petition to Determine Succession of Real Property. Although the mechanisms described above are not complicated, certain procedures must be followed. To save time and money, you should consult with an estate-planning attorney.

Certain assets are not subject to probate. For example, property passing to a surviving spouse because it was titled in Joint Tenancy: Community Property with Rights of Survivorship is not part of your probate estate. Neither are proceeds of life insurance policies when the named beneficiary is still alive. Other assets that avoid probate, as long as they have a valid designated beneficiary, include pension plans, IRAs, 403(b)s, 401(k)s, 457(b)s, U.S. savings bonds, and pay-on-death, or POD, accounts. Totten trust accounts and property titled in a living trust also are not subject to probate.

Tangible personal property, such as registered vehicles, mobile homes, truck campers, and boats, would be subject to the probate process only if your other assets exceed $150,000, thus causing your estate to be administered through court-supervised probate.

A will is less expensive, but factors other than cost may persuade you to invest in a living trust. Probating a will in California can be extremely expensive if the probate attorney's fees are based on the Statutory Fees and Commission schedule instead of a flat rate or an hourly rate. In addition, your attorney may request extraordinary fees billed at their normal hourly rate if they assist with the sale of real property or help to deal with a difficult heir and/or beneficiary. It can take up to a year or more to complete the probate process, and then the details become public record. This means that all your personal information, the names and addresses of your children, the nature and value of your financial holdings, and intimate thoughts conveyed in your will are revealed.

Whether you decide to use a will or a living trust, you will need to nominate a trusted individual to make decisions for you during a period of physical and/or mental incapacity. This is normally done by signing a well-thought-out advanced health care directive and financial powers of attorney.

In some rare situations, you may want your assets distributed under court supervision. Discuss this subject with your attorney to learn the pros and cons and whether this approach would suit your needs.

There is a series of logical steps that you should take in order to simplify what would otherwise be a difficult process: (1) create an accurate inventory of assets, including estimated value of real property, life insurance, financial accounts, and tangible personal property; (2) determine if a will or a living trust is going to be the best option to achieve your estate-planning objectives; (3) decide who will be your beneficiaries (see Chapter 21 for information regarding naming beneficiaries); (4) specify contingent/secondary beneficiaries; (5) choose at least two persons—if possible, three—whom you trust to carry out your wishes; (6) find a qualified estate-planning/trust attorney; (7) have your attorney prepare your documents, then sign them, which includes having them witnessed and notarized while signing; (8) transfer your assets into your name as trustee of your living trust; and (9) review your estate documents at the same time each year.

Another reason for choosing a living trust is the desire to control, from the grave, the legacy you spent a lifetime building. Preventing control from passing to beneficiaries who have special needs or are spendthrifts may give you peace of mind.

Another strategy is to use the living trust to provide your children with broad control and access to money you are passing to them, but not enough control to subject trust assets to creditors and those who are prone to making their living bringing frivolous lawsuits against people with wealth.

Today the living trust is the most common vehicle used to transfer assets at death.

Warning! You read above that joint tenancy avoids probate. When someone dies and her or his property is titled in joint tenancy, the surviving joint tenant(s) take ownership. Some people try to outsmart the system by titling their property in joint tenancy with their children to avoid probate. Sounds clean. All done. No problem.

Do not do it.

Think about this. What would happen if any of the children are the subject of a lawsuit and there is a settlement or judgment against them while you are living? You could be in jeopardy of losing your home. It has happened. Not so clean after all.

Want more to think about? When your children inherit your property after your death without being on title, the entire property gets a "step-up-in-basis." That is tax talk. It means the property can be sold for its fair market value, and the children would not have to pay a capital gains tax. However, if the children are joint tenants, their interest does not get the step-up-in-basis.

Get professional help. It is complicated.

5

NEVER FORGET YOUR PASSWORD

5-Steps to a Better Digital Life

The Story

"GETTING BACK TO MY EXAMPLES, I don't want that to happen to us," he said gravely. "Ace told me that these stories are common, whether it's the husband or the wife who dies. If they weren't involved together in managing their financial life, they view this subject as a black hole. One they don't want to enter."

"Well, okay, I'm starting to get a better sense of what you're learning. The process is fascinating. Remembering everything he's teaching you must be a challenge. But getting back to your examples, what was the second one?"

Mark started to answer, then stopped. "First, I want to tell you something I just remembered," he said, then he flashed one of his big smiles at her. "Honey, just talking with you ignites my memory!"

A proud smile appeared on her face.

"The other night, he taught me an easy-to-remember system on how to create and recall passwords. It'll make our digital life much easier."

Lisa laughed. "You know I hate passwords. I hate having to remember them, enter them, hate everything about them. And you know I never use the word *hate*. Will this system take my hate away and make me love passwords?"

Mark was grinning. "It'll take the hate away, but I don't know about the love part. Maybe."

With anticipation, Lisa said, "Well, go ahead, make my day."

"Okay, listen up."

Mark gave her a detailed description, then asked, "What do you think?"

"You kidding? It sounds fantastic. I love it. It's simple. I *love* it. You're right, it's easy. Thank you. I love it, I love it."

Mark, shaking his head, said, "Remember what Little Grandma said: 'You don't love things. You love people.'"

"Yeah, okay, well, I deeply, deeply adore Ace's system. More important, though, what you have explained so far has made me realize these dreams of yours are extraordinary. You're learning good stuff, and it's helping us."

The Nitty-Gritty

The regulators refer to your name, address, Social Security number, and financial records as Personally Identifiable Information, or PII. Websites with PII must have strong passwords, and they should be changed every 90 days. The problem? The passwords that are tough to hack are often difficult to remember. To make matters worse, we are told that each website should have a different password. It is a nightmare.

No system works for everyone, but the following may help you solve this everyday problem.

Step 1 - Start by creating a master password using a combination of letters, numbers, and special characters in an order you will never forget. Never. An example would be to use a special character like the pound sign (#) and then add a series of letters and number combination that you will, again, never forget (I like using an old address). As an example, I will use 1451#ElmSt. Utilize a similar format as your master password for all websites that do not have PII.

Step 2 - For those websites that have PII, insert identifier initials or codes to distinguish and access each account. An easy-to-remember code would be to use the website's first three letters in either lowercase, uppercase, or a combination. An example of a master password for your American Express account would be 1251#ElmStame. This structure would eliminate confusion about using a different password with each website. Those with PII should be changed every 90 days.

Step 3 - The solution for that is simple. Add numbers indicating the quarter and the year in any position, for example, 1251#ElmStame317, for the third quarter of 2017.

Step 4 - To satisfy the 90-day rule, change the quarter and year each quarter. Also consider changing its position. No need to relearn a new password. All you need to do is change the date sequence you used.

Step 5 - You should list each website to which you have assigned a password and whether it has the quarter and year code. That is it. A simple process. Finally, be consistent, and think twice before using an online program to record your passwords.

It is not complicated.

6

INFORMATION OVERLOAD

Look to the Clouds

The Story

LISA APPEARED AS ENERGIZED ABOUT these new ideas as her husband.

"Your mind is going 100 miles an hour. But you told me Ace had two examples. What's the second one? I want to learn more."

"Yeah, okay. It was about a couple who had been long-standing clients of his. Susan, the wife, died after a short illness. Her husband, Alan, never wanted to attend meetings, but she had insisted. So when she passed, he knew what was going on with their dollar ducks. He even had a list of their websites and knew her passwords. Ace said Alan understood what their plan was designed to achieve. Therefore, the money part wasn't a burden.

"That's the reason Ace wants us involved together. If something happens to me, like a stroke or I die, you could take Jill, John, or both kids to each meeting. I would do the same thing, at least at the beginning."

"Okay, but what about single people?" she argued. "They don't have a wife or husband. What should they do?"

"That's a fair question. Ace told me that single people should have someone who could take over, especially to help them when they are elderly and when they may be slipping a bit. They should have someone they trust on their team. A family member if possible, and then as time passes, if necessary, that person could manage all their financial affairs."

Just as he finished, Lisa walked over from the stove. "Here you go. Ham and eggs, the way you like them. Eggs over medium at six o'clock, ham at ten, and your favorite roasted potatoes at two; nice and organized."

"Thank you," he said. "Looks great and smells delicious!"

Before diving into the food, he added, "You know, you just reminded me of something else Ace just taught me."

"What this time? Keep talking. Sounds like Ace has the wisdom of a modern-day Socrates."

As he ate, Mark explained a 21st-century way to organize their financial information and records.

The Nitty-Gritty

In his book *Information Anxiety*, Richard Saul Wurman tackles an important problem—the widening gap between what we understand and what we think we should understand.

When it comes to understanding your financial life, that gap can be as wide as the Grand Canyon. The confusion over what you truly *need* to understand and what you *think* you should understand can be attributed to the availability of too much information and the inability to easily access the need-to-know information. The former overwhelms the latter. The key words to remember are "need to know." Essential information is all you need to know or need to have available.

Having command and control of information in the 21st century includes cloud-based data storage and retrieval. It is a clever way to organize your important documents and details about your financial affairs. It is a secure, modern-day digital filing system. In a single location, you can record and save everything you consider important—day-to-day savings and checking accounts, investments, IRAs, credit cards balances, medical records, will and living trust, personal journals, balance sheets, cash-flow projections, tax returns, recorded family history. Everything valuable you want to save and organize can live in the cloud. Financial accounts are updated daily. All important documents and family information are organized and at your fingertips. This tool would give your family members vital access to important legal documents in the event of your disability or death.

Usually we tackle each financial decision independently from the others. But is that the right tactic? Having access to all your need-to-know information may cause you to alter a decision you might otherwise have made. You may make better decisions after analyzing the influence of relevant contributing factors—the-need-to-know data.

Your financial life is a puzzle. Each piece must be identified and examined carefully, and all the pieces must fit together precisely before they can become a complete, viable strategy. When you make a financial decision without considering all influencing factors, it may be a good decision on its own merit, but be a mistake.

Everyone suffers from information overload. It causes you to close your mind. So how can you win the battle with excessive information? You could decide to a use a monstrous three-ring binder to house all your life's need-to-know material.

Such a book would have all your information. Whenever you needed to make important life decisions, the need-to-know data would be at your fingertips.

This strategy is a nice idea, but not practical. Your monster book would weigh a ton, and you would not be able to carry it with you everywhere. Updating it daily would be impossible. Nonetheless, it would be wonderful if you could put your hands on critical information instantly.

Leave the three-ring binder behind, fast-forward to the 21st century. Today, technology has reduced the size and weight of that three-ring binder. It is smaller than your purse or briefcase. What is it? It is the Life Management Logic website available from your CFP®, a secure cloud that you can access from anywhere.

Does your bucket list include going to Rome to study Italian cooking? If you had a medical emergency while preparing fettuccine Alfredo and the medical personnel rushed you to Concordia hospital, all your medical records could be made available to the doctors.

If you lost your passport, you could access a digital copy.

Suppose you wanted to buy a new car, but you did not know what payment amount would be manageable. You could check your future cash flow projections on your secure personal financial website to see what you could manage. You can use those same projections to see if you are saving enough to fund your retirement.

If a fire damaged your home, you could provide the insurance company with videos and pictures from your digital vault.

All you need is a secure Wi-Fi connection to the Internet to be able to access what you need to know.

It is not complicated.

7

TAKE CONTROL

Hire a Pro

The Story

"THE EGGS ARE PERFECT," MARK said as he stood up to get another cup of coffee. "Do you want more?" he asked, waving the French press at her.

"Please."

He poured a cup for both. He knew he had captured Lisa's attention. She was asking questions that revealed her curiosity and awareness. He realized that if she decided to get involved—and he was pretty sure she would—she would take control and make it happen.

"Here you go, honey."

"Thanks."

Mark continued, "Ham and eggs and some

Columbian coffee to get my weekend started. Thank you, it never tasted so good."

She rolled her eyes. "You say that about every meal I make."

He laughed, but then Lisa got serious. "Mark, before we go further, I need to ask you another question."

"What's your question?"

"I'm excited about planning our retirement, but I think we're making a mistake . . ."

"Okay, what?"

"You said something about finding a retirement professional, not a stockbroker. That sounds like a smart idea. And I agree, we need skilled help. But how do we find the right person?"

Mark said, "Well, Ace said we should find a retirement planning professional who has clients like us."

"What does that mean, 'like us'?"

"It means the person we select shouldn't have clients like the billionaires of the world. We don't have mega millions. If people we interview have doctors or dentists as clients, they wouldn't be the perfect choice either. And we need to know how many clients they have."

Lisa said, "Yeah, wow, that makes sense. If they're loaded up with clients, it would be like going to the doctor—whirlwind."

"You got that right."

"Did Ace tell you what the right number would be? Did he give you a range?"

"Yeah, he told me that after extensive research, a British anthropologist concluded that there's a limit to how many relationships it's possible to maintain effectively."

"Did he give you a number?"

Mark took a deep breath—he wanted to get this right. "Ace said research determined that our brain's neocortex has a physiological limit that constrains the number of social relationships it can manage to about 150. The guy's name was Robin Dunbar, so he called it the 'Dunbar Number.' Dunbar also said that with personal friends included, the client number is around 100.

"It also depends on the clients' needs and complexity. People with millions are more complicated—we don't need someone who specializes in that. But our needs are more complex than, say, Jill or John's."

"Mark, how do you feel about asking them all those questions?"

"We shouldn't be shy about asking questions. We need to know if their clients are like us, with similar objectives, income, and asset levels. And we need to know if they're overloaded with clients. After all, the person we choose will be working for us . . . we'll be paying the bill.

"We are older and near retirement. We have more money and more complex needs than younger people. That's the reason Ace said we should find a CFP® who has been managing investor portfolios through a variety of market ups and downs. He emphasized, too, how important it is to have good chemistry."

Lisa asked, "Did he elaborate?"

"Yeah—he said we don't need to become vacation buddies, but we do have to look forward to meeting with whomever we choose. Then he said something else that struck me. He said that we should find a CFP® who has a mature practice."

"What does that imply?"

"Well, he described a mature practice as one that the CFP® has built over time. It's established and doesn't require the CFP® to spend time beating the bushes to get new people in the door."

Lisa said, "Yeah, I get it. They wouldn't have as much time to help us."

Mark spoke softly. "You're giving me that look again."

"I know. I'm wondering, what should the kids do? Their situation isn't like ours. They don't have as much money as we've saved. At least I don't think so."

Mark had an answer ready. "Ace said the kids should have a CFP® on their team. A younger one. I don't mean in age, but in experience as a CFP®. They usually accept all new clients. The kids' circumstances wouldn't be as complicated or require as much time. They would be a good match.

"Then he told me something else."

"Oh? What?"

Mark was excited. "He told me that we have a choice—find a CFP® at a big wirehouse or at a small independent boutique firm. Both have CFP®s, but there's a cultural difference between how the two deliver financial services—"

"Mark, sorry for interrupting, but Evelyn works for a big company. She's not a CFP®, I know, but should we switch to one there? They probably have them, don't you think?"

"Yeah, they must," he said. "That would be one option. However, it would be uncomfortable if we demanded they replace Evelyn with a CFP®. Maybe exploring other companies might make better sense."

Lisa had her thinking cap on. "You're right. We could

get a fresh start."

"Great idea. Ace gave me the impression we should check out both big and small firms to see which would serve our needs best. Think about this, having a CFP® at a big wirehouse might offer services that the little guys may not have available."

"Like what? And are you saying 'warehouse'?"

"I don't know, and no, I'm saying 'wirehouse.' That's what they call the big brokerage firms."

She looked perplexed. "Why do they call them that?"

"It's a name they got during the late 1800s. They owned or leased the telegraph lines to make wire trades. It was faster. So they decided to call them wirehouses. The name just stuck."

Lisa, still confused, "Well, what services might the big wirehouses have that the, what did you call them, independent boutique firms don't have?"

"Ace didn't say. Maybe they're the same. I don't know. I guess that's something we need to find out. But he did give me some questions to think about and certain other key issues to explore before deciding whom to hire. He said to ask if their company has sales quotas. If they do, it places a negative influencing element into the relationship. Also, we should ask if they sell proprietary investments."

"What are those?" Lisa asked.

"They're investments created by the company. It would be better to buy a security created by a third party. We must be on the lookout and pay attention to the entire process.

"Another factor is, and get this, he said to ask if we'll be meeting with the owner. And if not, he told me we should find out if we would always be meeting with the same person or just get whomever was on the floor at the time and hopefully not some recent recruit."

Mark continued, "Whatever we do, we don't want to fall through the cracks because we picked the wrong group. Above all, Ace wants us to hire someone who doesn't have mandated, inflexible procedures that benefit them before us."

Lisa, once again reflecting, asked, "Do you think the small independent firms may be more flexible and more focused on us?"

Before Mark could answer, she changed course. "But isn't bigger better?"

"I don't know. Maybe not. Get this. I remember listening to a financial talk show a couple of years ago, driving home from the office. The host was emphatic— he said to get Wednesday's *Wall Street Journal*, the May 21, 2014, edition. He repeated the date so his listeners could take note. I don't know why, but I got the paper and read the article. It was titled 'More Brokers Break Away to Form Independent Firms,' and the subtitle was 'Trend Is Reshaping Industry, Eroding Dominance of Wall Street.' I decided to save it, and last week I dug it out and read it again. A research firm, Cerulli and Associates, said the number of independent advisers is increasing and the number of wirehouse advisers is shrinking.

"The article featured a broker that had been with a big wirehouse for more than 40 years, but decided he could serve his clients better if he formed his own independent firm."

Lisa suggested, "If small is better and that's the trend, maybe we should get an independent CFP®."

"Honey," he said earnestly, "we'll look at both. I think that's the way to make the best decision."

Lisa nodded her agreement. "How much do we pay Evelyn and her wirehouse?"

"That's a good question. I don't know. I know that nobody works without pay. But Evelyn has never given us any details about our cost or the commissions we're paying. If she did, it went over my head," he said, skimming his hand over the top of his head.

"Ace taught me something else about fees," Mark

continued. "He said there's something called an expense ratio. Each mutual fund manager charges that fee, and some have what's called a '12(b)1 fee.' We don't see those fees on our statements. Plus, there are transaction charges each time Evelyn buys or sells an investment. Lots of fees.

"And get this—I don't even know what expense ratios we're paying in our 401(k). I guess I'm not doing my job. That's going to change!"

Lisa declared, "Your friend Ace is right. We should get an advocate. Staying with Evelyn doesn't make sense to me. She has never given us a plan. Especially like what you're describing. And when she speaks, she uses words we don't understand—I think she's just telling us what her company tells her."

Mark noticed something big in Lisa's words, and it made him feel fantastic. She had referred to Ace as his friend. He considered that a breakthrough, a significant change. His confidence soared. It widened his constant smile.

"I like your attitude, honey. You're telling me that you want to make this happen. You're looking at positive action-based reasons to succeed, and that's what I need to hear."

The Nitty-Gritty

When you go out to get an ice cream sundae, you pick the closest store. If there are two nearby, you pick the one that you know is cheaper. After all, vanilla ice cream is vanilla ice cream.

There is a popular misconception that financial advisers are like vanilla ice cream. Pick the closest and the cheapest. Think again. Investigate further. Do not fall into that trap. People who offer investment and related services are very different—as different as Neapolitan and chocolate fudge. It is the same in every profession. Some are good, some are bad, and some are in between.

Your hunt for an ice cream parlor will be much easier than your hunt for a highly knowledgeable retirement planning professional. In the first instance, you want to satisfy your desire to experience quick pleasure. In the second, you want to increase your probability of enjoying lasting happiness.

Nosce te ipsum, know thyself. The building blocks for a hopeful future begin with knowledge. Do you know everything you need to know to prepare for your life when you retire? Probably not. So hire someone who does. There are times when we need the help that seasoned professionals can provide.

If you planned to climb Mount Everest, would you go to your local sporting goods store, purchase a tent, a lantern, some warm socks, and a few other supplies and then buy a ticket to Nepal? No, you would not—because you do not know what you need to know to climb that mountain.

Do you know what you need to know to climb Mount Retirement?

Learn from those who have helped others. Get a Mount Retirement Sherpa—a financial professional who can support you as you climb. Get a retirement planning professional.

Find a CFP® who has the experience, the knowledge, and the skill level to guide you. That person will be with you each step along the way. Her procedures may not be the same as those presented in this book, but that does not matter if she has a formal system.

You must explore your needs, wants, wishes, and obstacles. Each must be identified and examined thoroughly. As an independent, objective professional intermediary, your CFP® will help oversee your progress.

Obviously, you are not juggling daggers, but you are juggling all elements of your financial life. You need to consider your short-, intermediate-, and long-term goals. Remember this: you do not know what you do not know. Do not fool yourself into thinking that you do or that this book will be all you need. Know thyself. Hire a financial guide. You could learn new and valuable strategies.

Your search to find a CERTIFIED FINANCIAL PLANNER™ who is a retirement planning professional can start with asking relatives, friends, and coworkers about their experiences. This is not an easy task, but one that you should treat as an important early step. Do not jump the gun: finding "CFP®" after someone's name doesn't mean your search is over. That is where you start.

Remember: you have a choice in whom you hire. Before you decide, check out the ones you are considering. Websites are available to help you: www.CFP.net/search; www.plannersearch.org/; www.napfa.org;

www.finra.org/search; http://brokercheck.finra.org/; and
www.sec.gov.

You should also know that successful CFP®s have the luxury
of cherry-picking those they accept as clients. The good ones
have demanding schedules. Some work only with the mega
rich. To qualify, a new client must invest $5 million or more.
Some may not accept clients with less than $500,000. Meeting
that number is the starting point. The next phase is an
important one: Is the person someone you would want in your
corner? Do you feel positive vibes, and is there a good fit in
your eyes and the eyes of the CFP®? It's a two-way street. You
do not have to become best friends, but there must be an
attraction. If the chemistry does not feel right, keep searching.

Smart younger dreamers should be comfortable employing a
less experienced CFP®. Generally, younger people have less
complex needs. Therefore, experience is not as great a
consideration. Younger dreamers can benefit from the
knowledge that young, ambitious CFP®s have gained through an
extensive education, and they usually do not have minimums.

It is not complicated.

8

LESSON ONE

Visualize Happiness

The Story

WITH ANTICIPATION AND ENTHUSIASM, THE
Dolans completed their first lesson. They decided that if
they stayed healthy, their two-story dwelling would be
home forever. No downsizing or moving away from the
grandkids. Next came a key decision—the activities that
would replace Mark's work hours, eight hours each day.
This was a lot to replace. A new life. He realized that, at
the start, his "honey do" list would take a while to
complete. But when he finished Lisa's list, what then?
Maybe golf lessons. He and Lisa played occasionally, but
they had never taken formal lessons. It would be a way

to share time together.

Lisa wondered what it would be like to have Mark at home all day. She thought golfing would be a way to have time apart. Mark could have regular outings with his best friend, Charlie, who played every weekend.

She knew it was a cliché, but their "best friends" status added strength to their marriage. She believed that their love would deepen and intensify over the course of their retirement years. But she also believed that time apart would be important.

Their combined ideas were tangible evidence that Ace's instructions had worked.

Their vision became a collage of international and domestic travel. London's Tower Bridge, Paris's Eiffel Tower, the Colosseum in Rome, the Egyptian pyramids, Australia's outback. Washington, D.C., Colonial Williamsburg, Paul Revere's Boston, Mount Rushmore, the Golden Gate Bridge, the Grand Canyon. Seeing New England's fall colors and Civil War battlegrounds. Cruising in a paddleboat on the Mighty Mississippi. And everything in between.

They decided to take one international trip and one domestic trip each year. Vacation treks would be a top priority, at least during the first ten years, and maybe beyond, depending on their health.

To have some fun, they picked up paper and pencil and separately listed the countries they wanted to see. When they compared, Italy was number one on both lists.

Mark's man cave, a small bedroom he used as an office, was lined with bookshelves filled with classics that he had always said he would read when he retired. He knew he would really enjoy this reading, and it was an activity he was going to prioritize. His goal was going to be two masterworks each month.

Although Lisa and Mark occasionally went to a health club, they knew it should be more, and they decided not to wait nine years to implement a more regular schedule. They also decided to hire a physical fitness instructor, a professional who would put them on a proper program to develop cardiovascular endurance, strength, and flexibility, as well as offer suggestions on proper dietary habits. They wanted to be ready for all the traveling, and they wanted to be active well into their senior years.

Mark also harbored a secret desire—he had always wanted to be more proficient in the kitchen. He knew he had limited skills, so culinary classes would be on his list. It would be fun, and Lisa could join him.

Ace's lesson structure didn't require them to work

together. Each could let their imagination roam freely. Then later, they would compare their ideas and put the finishing touches on their plan. Plus, they knew they could modify it whenever and however they wanted.

Planning their new life produced positive feelings. Still, a nagging thought persisted in the back of Mark's mind. Evelyn managed some of their investments, but he had been managing the accounts she did not know about. Should he try to do all? No. His dreams had taught him otherwise. That would be foolish. This part of life is too problematic. Ace's instruction to hire a trained professional made sense, even for two Stanford grads.

The Nitty-Gritty

The following is based on a true story about a do-it-yourself investor. Names and details have been changed. Chico Jetton, CFP®, whom you will get to know better in a later chapter, recounts what happened one afternoon.

* * *

It was getting late on Thursday. Time for Sherrie and me to straighten up, lock the doors of Chico Jetton Retirement, Inc., and go home. The phone began ringing just as we started walking out the door.

"Do we need to answer that, Chico?" asked Sherrie.

"I'll get it," I said.

A man introduced himself, saying, "My name is Joe, and a friend said I must talk to you. I need a financial adviser. It's important."

His voice was soft, but conveyed fear and desperation. Nervously, he said, "I have to meet with you as soon as humanly possible."

Experience had taught me that this wasn't the time to pose the "why" question. Instead, I asked him to hold and gave the phone to Sherrie. I winked, nodded my head, and said, "Tell him 8:30 tomorrow morning."

The truth is, my regular routine never got me to the office by that hour. My first client visit of the day was always scheduled for 10:15 a.m. I only saw clients on Tuesdays, Wednesdays, and Thursdays. Besides that, I was always booked three weeks in advance. But this call touched me. I sensed a man in need, an urgent situation.

After the soft voice on the phone, Joe was a surprise. He looked like a retired football player. Broad shoulders, a couple of inches taller than me—maybe 6'4"—and probably 250 pounds. Lots of brown wavy hair for a man his age, which I guessed to be about 68. His arms were full of folders. He put them on Sherrie's desk and then gave me a sincere handshake, gripping my hand with both of his, signifying a silent heartfelt thank-you, which I also saw in his eyes.

Every client has a unique story. Sure, there are similarities openly etched on the surface. But deep within lies the rarely discussed truth. Everyone has that deeper secret. Joe had his.

He proceeded to tell me that after college graduation, he started working for his neighbor and friend, a plumbing contractor. Eight years later, his friend helped him start his own plumbing business. He described what sounded like a happy life.

Joe said, "I invested 35 years of blood, sweat, and tears building my company. I sold it seven years ago. I put the money from the sale into the account you're looking at. I started playing with stocks way back, maybe 20 years ago. I've done a good job, I think. Maybe. Okay, I gotta be honest. I really don't know how I've done. I've made money over the years, but compared with what? I don't know. Of course, I've lost money, too. Everyone does, right?"

In each client meeting, I try to read between the lines. Sometimes people don't say what they mean or what they want to tell you. There is an unspoken message underlying their words and facial expressions. I kept listening and looking for Joe's. I asked if he was married. He said yes and that they had been married for six years, adding that his first wife had died in a car crash a number of years ago. He told me he loved his wife, but didn't want her to attend our meetings because he wanted to keep the financial stuff to himself. She didn't know his net worth. He didn't want her to.

When scheduling appointments, Sherrie allocated two hours for each client visit. But I ended up needing nearly four hours to review all the information in Joe's folders. Good thing it was Friday—no other appointments. Timing is everything.

This relationship had started differently from others. He had come to me with the layers of his whole life in a pile of files, without being asked. He had everything. When I posed a question, he would start searching through his pile for the answer. And the answers were all there, concealed, waiting to be found.

We had three meetings to discuss his situation and possible strategies. At the end of the third meeting, he scheduled a

10:15 a.m. appointment for the following Tuesday to open his accounts.

All paperwork had been prepared, and Joe was on time. After some small talk, I review his paperwork with him. He started to sign the first application, then stopped, picked it up, and stared at it. His thoughts appeared to be somewhere else. After what seemed to me like an extended period of uncomfortable silence, I asked, "What are you thinking?"

Joe looked at me expressionlessly. "Before I left home this morning, Miriam asked me why I decided to pay someone to do what I've been doing for 20 years."

"What did you say?"

"Just because I'd been doing it that long didn't mean I know what I'm doing."

I waited for him to continue. He didn't.

My brain kicked in, and I said, "Joe, I don't want to be a party to marital problems. Better to iron this out before we go further."

He continued to stare at the paper without saying anything. Then picked up the pen and said, "This is what I want to do, and I need your help. She'll understand."

It took three more sessions to complete the seven steps in my L.I.F.E. Formula—Live. Imagine. Focus. Enjoy.®—and get Joe's financial ducks all in a row. His investments were mostly a portfolio of stocks and municipal bonds. He had adequate insurance to protect his assets. I set him up with a Life Management Logic web portal. The secure cloud gave him daily access to all his accounts, including savings and checking. He could look at his credit card balances every day to monitor against identity theft. His legal documents were stored in his digital vault for safekeeping and easy access.

The only problem I uncovered was with the IRS. And it was serious. Joe was older than I thought, 72 and had never taken his required withdrawal from his IRA account. The penalty is an additional excise tax of 50 percent. In his case, it was a lot of money. After discussing his circumstances, I had his CPA prepare IRS Form 5329. A letter was attached to explain why the institution holding the IRA didn't distribute the required amount the first two years. It made clear that the correct amount had been withdrawn when the mistake was discovered and that the mistake would not be repeated. The letter asked to waive the penalty tax.

Joe's plan required a timed harvesting of capital gains to offset considerable capital losses. Unfortunately, he had more losses than gains. After an extensive analysis of each company's prospects, we decided to wait until gains in his portfolio increased before selling the losers.

Three months passed, and I was happy to see Joe's name on the calendar. It would be his first quarterly review.

Concern gripped me when I saw him. He had lost a lot of weight. We sat together in the conference room, and I asked, "How are things?" His answer turned out to be his secret.

He didn't look at me. He looked through me and calmly said, "Chico, I'm going to die. I have less than three months. Inoperable brain cancer."

Joe had confided everything but this. I was stunned. And I couldn't help myself—tears started running down my cheeks.

Joe reassured me. "It's okay, Chico. You've helped me get everything in order. That's what I needed. You've done your part. Thank you."

At that point, my professionalism made me set aside my emotions. This new information changed everything. His plan wasn't finished. There was more work to be done.

I knew that no one, including the children, would get the advantage of deducting the losses on his stocks after he died. His IRA and living trust gifted everything to his two daughters, his son, and his wife in equal shares. Other than the IRA, his tax basis in the stocks would be the fair market value on the day he died. His losses died the same day. That's tax law. However, I knew something else, a little-known technicality. I could save the losses for Miriam. But it was complicated.

After reviewing details of what I needed to do for him, I called to schedule another meeting to describe my plan. He told me he wasn't physically able to come to the office. We scheduled a time for Sherrie and me to visit him at home.

I knew it would be the most stressful and demanding meeting of my 30-plus years in this profession. Joe was sitting in the living room, hooked up to oxygen. His appearance left little doubt that the end was near. Miriam sat all the way across the room. She didn't say anything after hello.

Presenting tax law under any circumstances is never easy. This was much worse. The plan I devised distributed his assets equally, but the secret in the sauce gave Miriam the benefit of all the losses to be used in the future as her stocks increased in value. I used an IRS bonus hidden in the Tax Code. Joe understood and wanted to get started. He said, "Yes, Chico, I want to do what you've suggested. Thank you. It'll help Miriam. Please get it done for me as soon as possible."

I did.

It is complicated.

9

FRIENDS ARE INDISPENSABLE

Source of Strength

The Story

LISA HEARD THE CLACKING SOUND coming from the chain-driven automatic garage door and knew her man had returned from the hunt.

Mark, with his ever-present smile, said, "Hi, honey, how was your day?"

After giving him a quick customary kiss, she said, "Busy! How was yours?"

Mark, still smiling, said, "I have the best news. We got the contract that Charlie and I have been working on for six months. We'll be getting a nice bonus next quarter."

Financial Principles Simplified

***

It was a hot June day 24 years ago when Mark and Lisa Dolan met Charlie and Doris Hatcher. Summer vacation had started. A perfect time to get away and have some fantasy fun. The families lived near each other, and their children attended the same school, but they had never met until an eventful day at Disneyland some 400 miles from home.

The parents watched as their children had boarded the Ferris wheel and enjoyed a couple of turns, when suddenly, the sound of grinding metal filled the air and the ride came to a screeching halt. The operator had mistakenly pushed the wrong lever at a critical moment. The Dolan kids teetered in the swinging seat at the top. The Hatcher kids were one seat behind.

The panic-stricken parents somehow remained calm, trying not to cause alarm because the children did not know the wheel was stuck. Within moments, security and maintenance staff appeared. The park manager advised the frightened parents that it would take only a few minutes to go through the process to reset the gears, fix the problem, and restart the wheel.

Waiting anxiously, all the parents started talking to one another. Doris was crying, and Charlie was trying his best to convince her that the kids would be okay.

Lisa walked over and offered Doris a bottle of water, hoping to comfort her.

Then they heard the motor roar to life, and what had seemed like an endless wait was finally over. The Ferris wheel turned slowly, stopping to release its precious cargos two by two.

Relieved and happy, the Dolans and Hatchers started talking to one another. To their surprise, they discovered that they lived in the same neighborhood, only blocks apart, and their little ones had the same teacher. They hit it off immediately, all of them commenting on what a small world it was.

Without either suggesting it, they spent the day together, following their children from ride to ride and taking breaks to have lunch and dinner together.

After the fireworks display, they exchanged contact information and set a date night for the following week. A mishap had launched a wonderful, enduring friendship.

Mark and Charlie developed a rare bond. They even ended up working at the same company.

Lisa and Doris also became close friends, enjoying common activities and supporting each other through the ups and downs of life as mothers and wives.

***

"Well, congratulations! How much?"

"There's no way to figure it out until the dust settles and the transaction is completed," he said. "But it could be as much as a month's pay."

"What are we going to do with the extra money? Add it to our retirement account?" she asked.

"Of course—even though it would be nice to expand our summer vacation plans."

"Mark, you make me proud. You've been working hard to get that contract, and to put the extra money toward our retirement demonstrates your commitment."

"Thank you," he said, giving her a hug. Then he surprised her. "I know I said that getting that contract was the best news, but I misspoke."

"Misspoke? How?"

"No question that getting the contract is great news. But I have better news."

"What could be better?"

"Well, Charlie and I went to Mexican Paradise to celebrate."

"I know, your favorite place to satisfy your midday cravings. By the way, have you said anything to him about Ace?"

"Yeah, I did. That's what I want to tell you. I wasn't sure how to go about it, so I just decided to plunge in. I explained every dream, as best I could. I told him how they started and what I've learned. Then I told him that we had decided to get a CFP® to help us develop a full-scale plan."

"What did he say?"

"About the CFP®?

"No. I mean yes. I mean about everything."

"He surprised me. He didn't say a word while I talked. And when I finished, he just looked at me. It seemed like an eternity. Then he said, 'Mark, I've known you 24 years, and I know you well. Your story is preposterous. Think about it. How could a real person come to you in your dreams? But you know what? I'm cool with it. Plus, I'm no dummy. Anyhow, what you've told me is profound—fascinating, intriguing, insightful stuff. I want to learn more. If the dreams continue, keep me in the loop, okay? And your decision to get help sounds like it could be a key factor, although I don't know much about those people. I guess they're on the same level as CPAs and lawyers.'"

Mark looked at Lisa to see if she was taking it in. "He about knocked me off my feet, well, actually, off my seat, since I was sitting. Then he asked me a lot of good questions. Not like he was making fun or to see if I was spacing out. It was the opposite, in fact. I was surprised, but he wanted more details and wants to learn as much as possible if the dreams keep coming."

"Wow! Are you *sure* he wasn't having some fun at your expense?"

Mark shook his head. "You should've been there. He asked me to tell him about each dream. He even used Ace's name. He wants me to teach him everything I learn. Honestly, I thought I'd just freak him out, maybe even that he'd look at me like I had a screw loose—his reaction blew me away. He's a special guy."

"Did he say anything else?"

Mark got excited. "Get this, he said that Doris and he have been struggling with the same problem, and even though it has been a major issue, they haven't come up with a way to get started. And then he said, 'I get it. That's where the CFP® comes in.'"

"What else did you tell him?"

"I told him what I remembered about how to profile the CFP®, the ideas we talked about at breakfast. He had never heard about the fiduciary stuff. And I told him how to setup a master password. He liked that a lot, said it was a 'great idea.' I mentioned that Lesson One requires you to ask questions to reveal what you want life to give back and that your answers give birth to expanding your dreams, your ideas, and reaping life's rewards. That it's the same as setting goals."

Mark paused, then added, "You know, honey, there's something else he and I talked about that you and I haven't discussed."

"What?"

"When we dig deeper, we'll see that this process means being prepared for problems, the kind you never plan for. If glitches don't happen, that'll be great, but if they do, we must be prepared."

"Like what glitches? What are you thinking about?"

"The unexpected, of course, but also stuff we know happens, but don't plan for. Like high inflation—Ace said it was our number one enemy; and then there are health care costs and serious medical problems, like maybe Alzheimer's, helping the kids if bad things happen to them that they didn't plan for, putting a new roof on our house, an earthquake . . . you know, setbacks we know are out there, but don't know if or when they'll happen. I guess the biggest thing would be running out of money."

Lisa was listening and thinking about the magnitude and scope of everything that must be planned. She understood the importance of planning . . . but still, it was intimidating. She felt a tinge of renewed fear.

Shaking it off, she asked, "So Charlie seemed

excited?"

Mark shrugged. "Yeah, he kept hitting me with questions. Then he stopped and said his food was cold and asked Rosie to nuke his plate. But the expression on his face told me more. I know he doesn't think I'm crazy. He wants to get a plan, too—looks like we're not gonna be alone in this! Besides Ace, we have our best friends with us, as long as Doris sees things the way you and Charlie do. Won't that be fantastic?"

Then he said, "I've been learning a lot, and today I learned we got that contract.

"But more important, I learned that my friendship with Charlie is rarer than I thought. I love the guy," he exclaimed.

10

LESSON TWO

Asset Protection

The Story

LISA FELT SECURE WHEN SHE took control of the couple's common responsibilities. Maybe it was something innate or perhaps it was an instinct absorbed through growing up with parents who ignored their children's basic needs, lacked guiding principles and common sense, and had no idea how to provide family security.

This new idea about planning for retirement had made her uneasy at first, but now she knew it was time to take control, and that was her normal pattern. Mark had talked with her about Lesson Two, making sure they had protection for their assets and protection from financial loss. She needed to figure out how much protection they had and for what, and what they lacked.

When she went to Stanford, she had an off-campus apartment with two other young women. She had grabbed the bull by the horns, taking the initiative for basic responsibilities, including making sure they had the proper insurance contracts in place to protect their limited assets.

When she married Mark, she continued to oversee those same critical obligations, only on a bigger scale. Her childhood and college experiences made it an easy transition, and she found the role rewarding. It gave her comfort to know that if the unexpected happened, it would be a controlled disaster. It was an insurance company's money at risk, not hers.

Lisa felt confident when she started Lesson Two. She was familiar with the subject of asset protection, so she dove into an examination of their documents and other information their insurance agent had provided.

First, she read through the descriptions of regular reimbursement coverages—home, auto, umbrella liability. She wasn't sure about an umbrella contract or if they had it. Reading further, she realized that if they did not have it, they must consider it. She assumed their insurance agent had recommended adequate coverage, but she knew she should never assume . . . she needed confirmation.

Then she moved on to personal protection: life, medical, disability income replacement, dental, and vision coverage.

She went online to check Mark's benefits package at work to see if she had missed anything. She had. His choices included an option to add inexpensive supplemental life coverage equal to two times his annual income. She knew that would be good to have, but needed to wait until April for the open enrollment period. She added a note to her iPhone.

The rest was current. Mark had income continuation until age 65 if he became permanently disabled. His major medical had unlimited coverage with no restrictions on doctors.

Something else caught her attention. His plan had an option to pick up convalescence and nursing home benefits for later in life. She had never thought about coverage for long-term care, but decided they should discuss it and then talk with someone who could give them specific details.

The Nitty-Gritty

In Lesson One, you describe your wants, wishes, and possibilities. Lesson Two will help you tackle your asset protection needs and instruct you on ways to defend yourself from potential financial loss.

A brief study of this topic will reveal a whole range of concerns—unintended acts of negligence on the part of family members, death, disability, damage to home and other property, and poor health. When you have the wisdom to put your needs first, you can go wild with your wants.

At this point we need to face facts. Lesson Two is not fun. However, it is necessary. When it is completed, you will feel immense satisfaction from knowing you did the right thing, knowing you have guarded your family's financial future.

Your CFP® will help you coordinate the process of reviewing your assets and obligations and will alert you to any weaknesses that could cause a negative financial impact.

Your home, your automobile, and negligent acts are protected with casualty insurance. Both your home and your auto policies have limited liability coverage, but you can add, at a low cost, an umbrella liability contract.

An umbrella contract insures your assets when you or a family member commits certain unintended careless acts. If you have an at-fault liability outcome and do not have adequate coverage, you may have to use your savings, sell an asset, or liquidate your after-tax retirement accounts to pay a settlement or judgment. A low-cost umbrella liability policy for $1 million or more will give you needed protection and peace of mind.

Medical insurance is also essential. Your family could

become destitute if you neglect this responsibility.

If you are in your peak earning years, you should consider safeguarding your ability to earn money with disability insurance. When you cannot work because of an accident or a serious illness, this contract will replace your paychecks so you can pay your bills and continue to fund your savings for retirement.

Asset protection includes shielding your retirement accounts from loss. You may have two categories of retirement assets. Qualified retirement plans, also known as ERISA plans, have unlimited creditor and bankruptcy protection. Qualified assets are before tax, that is, they still contain the tax element. These include pension, profit sharing, and 401(k) plans, some 403(b) plans, and others.

This can get tricky, though. You need to be aware that when a 401(k) plan is rolled over to an IRA, although it retains the same bankruptcy protection, it does not retain creditor protection. You should also know that traditional IRAs are treated differently than IRA rollovers from 401(k) plans, because they have limited protection from bankruptcy—in 2016, the maximum amount protected is $1,283,025. This amount adjusts based on the Consumer Price Index and may change every three years. Generally, rules vary from state to state.

After-tax investments are unprotected—they are available to creditors and are not protected in bankruptcy proceedings.

Next, take a hard, objective look at your life insurance portfolio. What are the odds? It doesn't matter. What matters is this: Could death occur before your treasure chest is full? You know the answer. Even ancient Romans recognized the importance of life insurance. They had "burial clubs" to cover members' funeral costs and assist survivors financially.

Ask the wealthy, wise, and well informed, and they will tell you that life insurance is a treasure. They know they are providing a chest full of money for the ones they love. It will replace the money they would have earned if they had lived. It is part of a family's dignity and financial strength. The pain of paying premiums is overpowered by the sweet comfort of providing for loved ones.

An intellectual study of the possible death of either head of a family will reveal two main setbacks—emotional and financial. The emotional damage will heal over time. The financial damage may never heal. A death will cause the financial engine to stop pumping money into your treasure chest. The flow of money can continue only if a replacement pump is provided in advance. Insurance.

Protect your family. Keep your family's income flowing. Make a big company assume your high-risk exposure. Having life insurance is proof positive of your good judgment and your commitment to caring for your loved ones.

Another negative financial risk is possible convalescent care cost when you are older. Long-term-care contracts are expensive, but necessary if you want to safeguard your possessions and provide a family legacy. The younger you are when you secure coverage, the lower the premium. I would advise tackling this task no later than your 50th birthday. I did not and was diagnosed with prostate cancer at age 53. When I applied for coverage I was declined. I waited too long. Do not make the same mistake.

If you have an employer, check with your human resources

department to learn if low-cost benefits and add-ons are available. Supplemental life insurance is cost-effective. The additional accidental death rider is not as valuable because you need to die within a certain period, although there is nothing wrong with having it as long as the added cost does not prevent you from securing other, more valuable protection.

If you are self-employed or work for a firm that does not provide employee benefits, you have a bigger financial burden. You must dig deeper to use good judgment.

In order to be able to assist you with all of this, your CFP® must have at least a basic knowledge of employer benefits packages and personal insurance contracts, including auto, home, life, liability, and health.

She must also have a good working knowledge of the income tax code and the tax rules on IRAs and other retirement accounts. Taxes are a huge factor. Plus, violating the rules on tax-deferred accounts, like 401(k) plans and IRAs, can jeopardize tax-sheltering benefits and potentially cause stiff penalties. Violate just a couple of the rules—maybe even just one of the rules—and the entire account could be taxed, destroying its long-term tax advantage. Knowing the ins and outs may help you save money, not to mention misery. To reduce your exposure to loss, you will want a CFP® who knows her way around IRS Publication 590, Parts A and B.

Finally, you need to evaluate whether you should update all your legal documents, including your will, living trust, and financial and health powers of attorney. But, you ask, how do I update what I don't have? If this sounds like you, talk to a qualified CFP® to learn why you need these estate-planning documents and how to find a qualified trust attorney who will help you get this money duck in line with the others. Having these documents in place is an extremely important family responsibility.

At this stage, you might benefit by rereading Chapter 4, on estate planning.

A 2016 online survey of 2,000 adults aged 18 and over, conducted by Harris Poll for Rocket Lawyer, found that 64 percent did not have a will. Their reason? They had not gotten around to it.

The multitalented artist Prince apparently never got around to it. His sister filed papers in court claiming he died without a will. President Abraham Lincoln knew there was a group that wanted to assassinate him. But, surprisingly, he didn't have a will and he was a lawyer.

Why do adults neglect this important responsibility? It is because nobody expects to die. If this shoe fits, do not rationalize, do not offer excuses—and do not put off this obligation any longer. Just get it done. Make a will. It will make you feel proud.

Even better than getting just a will, also get a living trust and financial and health care powers of attorney. The living trust, if done properly, will avoid the dreaded costly and time-consuming probate process, not to mention the publicity. You may not be Prince, but do you want everyone in your hometown to know the personal details of your financial life? A living trust is not an expense. It is an investment to protect those you love as well as your legacy.

A Group 1 person will recognize not only the need for protecting assets, but also the best and most immediate solution. The Group 2 person will see the same truths, but will

look for excuses or reasons to avoid taking action.
But it must be done. It is complicated.

11

MEETING OF THE MINDS

Strong and Modern Women

The Story

AS LISA TURNED THE CORNER with her grocery cart to explore the frozen food aisle, she banged into Doris Hatcher.

"Sorry! Hey, fancy meeting you here," Doris laughed.

"Hi, Doris. How are you?"

"Surprised to learn that my best friends are cajoling my husband into believing people's dreams have any validity."

"Oh, yeah, that. How much has Charlie told you?"

"A lot. Extensive details. Whenever they talk, Charlie comes home, writes everything down in a notebook, then tells me.

"He said it's as though Mark's having conversations with a real person—when he's sleeping! I'm wondering if you two got your hands on some of those 'special' brownies that California made legal. Are you guys hallucinating?"

Doris had a big smile on her face, but she was making a point, and Lisa understood. She did not know whether to discuss the dreams. She thought she should defend them, but was not confident she could. Then without a deliberate decision on her part, she heard herself talking.

"Believe me, Doris, I get your point. When Mark told me about his dreams, I had the same thoughts—well, maybe not about the brownies," she chuckled. "But after more dreams and more conversations with him, it didn't matter to me where the ideas came from. What mattered was that he had started to do something that I've been reluctant to even think about or talk about, let alone do anything about. The dreams are helping me, helping us. We've had a lot of these conversations, and his dreams really are conveying complete and intelligent thoughts on this subject. How he gained this wisdom doesn't matter, at least not to me. He and I have made a promise to each other to use this extraordinary event as the spark we needed to get our life in order. It doesn't make sense to continue going aimlessly from day to day, hoping things will go our way. I'm thrilled that we're starting to do something positive to shape our future. We've completed two lessons. Who knows, maybe Mark has a telepathic connection to a real person! But honestly, it just doesn't matter."

"Okay, Lisa. I hope I didn't sound rude. If I did, I'm sorry. You're making your point clear. I guess I should keep an open mind. You're right—it shouldn't make any difference where the ideas came from if they're providing you with the foundation for creating what you want your retirement to look like. To be honest, I'm impressed with your . . . innate logic."

Lisa sensed Doris needed, actually wanted more details. She decided they should talk further.

"Doris, are you in a hurry?"

"No."

"Well, then, let's check out and go to the coffee shop. I can give you my take on why I believe Mark's dreams are an omen."

* * *

Doris and Charlie Hatcher had impromptu discussions about retirement. However, their discussions had centered on the abstract. They had never made any concrete decisions. They did not know how.

Then Charlie had started sharing with Doris everything that he was learning from Mark. She had a good understanding of what Mark's dreams were about and was a little astonished at the detail. It made her wonder if it really might be a human communicating with Mark. How could that be? She did not have an answer. But . . . did it matter?

Nevertheless, Doris had decided that Charlie's involvement with Mark's fantasy, visions—or maybe hopeful aspirations would be a better description— would be his and Mark's thing, not her and Charlie's thing.

Then she remembered she had told Lisa she would keep an open mind, and she started thinking about their talk over coffee, about the dreams and retirement. Oh, well, it was time to head to the gym.

As she drove, serious thoughts were racing through her mind. She wondered whether the substance of Mark's dreams could be major, life-altering. She and Charlie did not have a plan. Mark could be studying something useful. She smiled as she realized she was arguing both sides.

Lisa had made an excellent point—the source of the ideas didn't matter. So what did? The subject. It was of great consequence and just might help Charlie and her have a better life. Her mind kept returning to that thought.

As she turned into the parking garage, she noticed the bus across the street with a lot of gray-haired people lining up. Where were they all going? She saw a sign: International Airport Express.

They're probably retired, she thought. Then she started wondering: *Where will they land? Rome, London, Paris? All three? Had they planned their retirement? Did they have all their "dollar ducks in a row," as Charlie kept repeating? Did they have their plan on paper, plus a digital copy accessible from anywhere in the world? Could they check on their portfolio and credit card balances while in Paris? Did they have peace of mind? Were they confident that the unexpected wouldn't throw them for a loop?*

Doris felt like a total, strong woman of today when she was exercising, and this led her to reflect on the problem at hand. *Am I being strong and modern by ignoring this problem? But maybe it's not a problem, maybe it's only a problem in my mind.* She was watching from a distance as her best friends made plans with the assistance of a person who did not exist. *Was it possible that Lisa was right, that Mark had an actual clairvoyant connection to a real person? Could that really explain his dreams? Could that even be?*

Maybe it would be best not to get too involved. Or should she join their fun? She was confused, puzzled, uncertain, wavering between yes and no. As her mind searched to find answers, a scary thought hit her. Remembering Charlie's description of Group 1 and Group 2 people, she wondered if she could be a Group 2 person. No, not possible! She did not want to be in that group! That was the precise moment when she made her decision—she would help Charlie with what he said a Group 1 person would do.

To her amazement, she decided the Dolans and Charlie could be on to something that appeared to be more good than bad, something that should not be ignored.

Doris wished Charlie had never told her that Ace came from Mark's dreams. She would have felt better if she thought Ace was a real person Mark had hired. But after thinking further, she realized that Lisa was right—it truly did not matter.

Knowing what your life should look like after you retire suddenly made sense to her. They must make plans, take some steps to get them where they wanted to go. She knew that was the smart thing to do. The Dolans would help—she and Charlie were very lucky to have such wonderful friends.

12

LIVE TO 105?

Life Expectancy vs. Longevity

The Story

THE DOLANS EXPECTED TO RETIRE when Mark reached his 67th birthday. It seemed like the distant future, but time has a way of speeding by, like a bullet train. They knew that the day would be upon them sooner rather than later, and they did not want any negative surprises. They needed to do whatever was necessary to have enough money to live the good life. Their ideas about what retirement life ought to be were becoming more vivid.

Mark knew he wanted his first sunrise after work to materialize by design and be an orderly transition to a new, exciting real-life dream come true. He did not want the dawning of this new life to happen simply by accident, a pileup of random, unrelated events and calamities.

But now it was time for bed. Mark laid his head on his pillow and drifted off to sleep. As his slumber deepened, his dreams were commanding him to take control. Ace had taught him that it would be a mistake to expect everything to flow together without human intervention. A confident smile appeared on his peaceful face as his mind reflected on his life and on what he had recently learned.

He had plotted his life's course carefully and thoughtfully thus far. The right college, the right connections, the right career path. There are well-intentioned adults who essentially live day to day. They expect life to advance without any effort on their part. But even as a young man, Mark knew a central truth—that line of thinking could backfire. More often than not, the future is packed with anxieties and struggles.

So saving money regularly over the years had been important. Maybe it was a habit he and Lisa had picked up from their parents and grandparents, when listening to them talk about the Great Depression. Whatever the reason, they knew this—having money salted away and instantly available gave them a feeling of power and control.

Their purchasing decisions had been part of this good habit. Whenever they had needed a new car, they would contemplate buying a fancier model, but then one of them would point out that the more basic model would get the job done and they could save the extra money— umbrella money, they called it—in case of a rainy day. They also saved "tax smart" money from every paycheck by contributing to a 401(k).

Mark and Lisa had prepared for their life before retirement, and both now knew they had to be ready for their life after retirement. Retirement was equally as important and possibly fraught with more pitfalls. They wanted their life in retirement to be a textbook picture of fun and gratification, not something that looked like a 1960s psychedelic tie-dyed shirt. They would mix the colors their way.

The recurring dreams had inspired Mark to embrace a life-changing reunion with active thinking. Ace had taught him that even when it comes to retirement, the world has two kinds of people: those who make things happen and those who let things happen—people who control life, and people who let life control them. But Ace had also shown him that those who allow life to control them could experience a positive transformation through conscious and concerted effort.

Mark had decided he would be a Group 1 achiever. He had also made another important decision. He would not put off getting professional help—it just made sense. Plus, he must have Lisa as an equal partner, working and planning with him. He knew that her retirement dreams probably did not match his, but he realized that it did not matter. And he knew he could not plan their retirement without her. It was, after all, *their* retirement.

The dreams were providing direction. Mark realized that there would be good times—some super good—and difficult times. People say that you have to take the good with the bad, but his lessons had taught him that that is not true. Ace had convinced him that he could have a positive influence over his future. He understood there must be commitment, calculated action, and follow-through. He did not want to make a senseless mistake that could have been avoided.

Mark awakened with enriched conviction and a smile of satisfaction. A smile Ace had put there. His favorite aroma was wafting into the bedroom, and without opening his eyes, he knew Lisa had already made her way to the kitchen.

As Mark placed a loving kiss on her cheek, she said, "Well, good morning. Did anything happen last night?"

"Yeah, Ace was with me. I'm excited. Not only have we made a pledge to ourselves, but also, Ace has reinforced his pledge to us—to guide us along the way. We're a team."

"Well, tell me more."

"Get this. Last night's dream gave me a strong sense of excitement—I realized that we have to plan a long life. We could live to be 100. Believe it! 100 years old!"

That gave Lisa pause. "I don't know, live to 100? I don't know. Do you think that's possible?"

The Nitty-Gritty

A famous comedian said, "I have all the money I will ever need . . . if I die tomorrow." She was no dummy. She realized that to determine how much money she would need, she needed to know how long she would live. If she had a husband, she needed to know how long he would live.

As of this writing, Norman Lloyd, actor, producer, and director, is 100; David Rockefeller, banker and philanthropist, is 99; Olivia de Havilland, English-American actress, and Kirk Douglas, American film and stage actor, film producer, and author, are both 98; Zsa Zsa Gabor, Hungarian-born American socialite and actress, is 97; Billy Graham, American Christian evangelist, is 96; Carol Channing, American actress, singer, dancer, comedian, and voice artist, and Hugh Downs, longtime American broadcaster, television host, news anchor, TV producer, author, game show host, and music composer, are both 93. The list goes on.

The amazing Harriett Thompson, age 92, has set a record as the oldest woman to finish a marathon. She did it at San Diego's Rock 'n' Roll Marathon on May 31, 2015. Wall Street stockbroker Irene Bergman turned 100 in August 2015 and was still managing clients' portfolios.

Some experts recommend that you plan on living until somewhere around age 105. Whew. That's old, huh?

Sir Nicholas George Winton, British humanitarian, celebrated his 105th birthday on May 19, 2014. At his party, Winton said, "As far as I am concerned, it is only anno Domini [time] that I am fighting—I am not ill, I am just old and doddery [shaky]." He turned in his driver's license at age 99.

How long should you plan on living? Usually you would get your answer from a mortality table. According to the Social Security Actuarial Life Table, a 65-year-old female's life expectancy is to age 86.6; a male to 84.3.

The Social Security Administration's research says that some people will live longer than the "average" retiree and that women tend to live longer than men. About one of every four females now 65 years old will live past age 90, and more than one out of 10 will live past age 95.

Do you want your bank account empty at the age the life expectancy table says you are supposed to die? Absolutely not—that would be a disaster plan. One of the most intense fears you can experience is running out of money. That fear becomes magnified when you retire. If you run out of money and are still alive, what would you do? Your options are limited, and none are attractive. Save your money. Build and grow a massive "money machine."

Caution! Life expectancy and longevity are different. Life expectancy focuses on how long an individual of your age, gender, and health status would be expected to live on average. Longevity focuses on how long you will live. Notice that in the list above, each person's longevity has taken her or him beyond life expectancy. Save money for a long life. Be prepared.

It is not complicated.

13

SOCIAL SECURITY

Will You Get Yours?

The Story

MARK CONTINUED, "WE *COULD* LIVE to 100. We're healthy. My parents are in their 80s, and they still have an active lifestyle. Your grandparents lived into their late 80s, and Papa and Little Grandma lived into their early 90s. So, yeah, it's definitely possible. And the breakthroughs coming out of medical research are mind-blowing. Seems like there's something new every day. Anyway, we should continue a healthy diet and stick with our commitment to hire a professional trainer so we can stay fit. My idol, George Burns, repeated a famous quote when he said, 'If I knew that I was going to live this long, I would've taken better care of myself.' He lived to 100, smoked a cigar, went to sleep, and his life ended. Gotta hand it to old George. He did it right."

Lisa said, "Well, it seems a little farfetched to me."

"Ace said that if we live to 100 and don't have enough money, we'd need to move in with the kids. That's not a happy thought . . ."

"No. That would be humiliating."

"We just need to prepare so that doesn't happen."

"Does Ace want us to plan to live that long?"

"Well, we should. Planning leads to happiness no matter what you do. It makes total sense, and I'm glad we're doing something positive. Completing the first two lessons has given me added confidence. Honey, I know my dreams are strange, but how are you feeling? Are you still excited?"

Lisa had been preparing breakfast and listening carefully. She had made up her mind about something she believed was pivotal. She accepted Ace as a real person, although she could not understand how a human could come to you when you are sleeping. He had never been in her dreams. Why not? She felt a twinge of the green-eyed monster.

Mark waited for her answer, patiently but intently, watching as she placed a plateful of piping hot blueberry pancakes on the table. She stopped, looked at his smiling face, and said, "Of course. I'm as committed as you are. But my level of confidence isn't the same. You're the one having the dreams. You're the one experiencing firsthand something that we can agree is, well, mysterious. But as crazy as it sounds, I'm with you. So if you're asking me, am I committed, the answer is a big yes. Working with you on the first two lessons gave me a strong sense of confidence. I'm in the dark about what comes next, though. That's why we need to find someone to help us. A person I can actually talk with."

Lisa was rewarded with one of Mark's biggest smiles. She could tell her words filled his heart with joy.

Mark knew at that precise moment that everything would be okay, no matter how much work they had to put into this challenge. He felt a heightened sense of eagerness and exhilaration, and his commitment and confidence grew. The air of anticipation was exciting.

Mark experienced vivid flashbacks of his dreams that added genuine substance and precision to his thinking. He felt confident they could make sure their future was as bright as possible. He made an unswerving personal pledge to get their dollar ducks organized.

Today was the day. There was no better time than right now to tackle this important life project. From this day forward, he would maximize each minute to the fullest. No time wasted. No excuses accepted. He would take control. He felt confident.

The Nitty-Gritty

Before your financial professional will be able to build your plan, she will need to know the answers to loads of questions. A big one is, how much guaranteed annual income will you receive as a percentage of expenses during retirement? She will add it up—pensions, Social Security, and annuity payments—to determine whether you have a spending deficit or surplus. The answer will give her a perspective on the best way to invest your retirement assets.

The most well-known form of guaranteed income is Social Security. According to the Social Security Administration (SSA), nearly nine out of ten individuals 65 and over receive benefits. The highest percentage of people start taking income at age 62, the lowest percentage of people wait till age 70. Which do you think is the smartest? It is a trick question because it is not the right question. The right question is, which is the smartest *for you?* It depends on your answers to a series of important questions. Planning your Social Security payment strategy must be done carefully. No quick decisions should be made here. But never fear. Your CFP® has your best answer in her computer.

There is a concern that the SSA is going broke. I must tell you that the depth of this subject is, without question, above my pay grade. Search online for the 2016 OASDI Trustees Report. It will give you some sense of how involved this operation is and why there is concern. The technical pieces are so complex that the only people who can understand the numbers are actuaries. Very intelligent people with a highly specialized education. They analyze a complicated set of factors: demographics, economics, beneficiaries, trust fund operations, and actuarial status.

But to help you understand the problem, consider this major point. In 1945, there were 45 workers paying into Social Security for every one beneficiary. It has been projected that in 2020 there will be fewer than three workers for each beneficiary. To help make up the difference, workers today are paying a much higher percentage of their compensation in Social Security taxes.

The OASDI Trustees Report makes a 75-year projection and is in three parts: low cost, intermediate and high cost. In the projection of low cost, the SSA does not run out of money. The report of intermediate cost is the one delivered to Congress. It projects that the SSA will run out of money in 2034 and that thereafter, only 79 percent of normal benefits will be paid, decreasing to 75 percent in 2090. The report outlining high cost projects that the SSA will run out of money in 2029.

The key question is: How do you plan? My opinion is that if you are 55 years of age or older, you can probably count on Social Security. My belief is that the middle-of-the-road projection is the worst-case scenario for this age group. Your CFP® will factor that reduction into your cash-flow projections. It is better to know than not to know. Continue to work with your CFP® and amend your plan when needed so that you are prepared for any negative event. And that event may be a nonevent. Remember Y2K?

What should you do if you are younger than 55? Three things. Plan, plan, and plan. Create a plan that does not include benefit payments from Social Security. When you prepare properly, you will have a better opportunity to achieve your desired outcome, and you may get your benefits—the proverbial icing on the cake.

Ben Franklin said, "In this world, nothing can be said to be certain except death and taxes." And we must be on guard for the rest, which brings to mind a Franklin quote you read in Chapter 2. "By failing to prepare, you are preparing to fail." As a Group 1 person, you will do what you must in order to reduce the bad and amplify the good. Your CFP® will be at your side, and she will prepare as many as 1,000 cash-flow projections to give you a visual sense of how your financial future will advance. I cannot stress this enough—it is better to know than to be in the dark. Those who know fare better than those who do not know.

The truth is that the stream of cash flow from Social Security could be massive, a treasure. Should you, like the majority, take Social Security income at age 62, along with a big haircut? Or should you delay until age 70 to get a 24 percent increase over your age 67 benefit? During your lifetime and, if you are married, the lifetime of your spouse, the difference could amount to thousands of dollars.

It is an easy decision, though, if you are single, if you are not working and need money, if you are in bad health, if you do not expect a long life, and do not have family obligations. If these factors apply to you, take the money at 62, if that is what you want. Like I said, easy. Otherwise, there is no quick answer. There are just too many variables. Your CFP® will need to calculate a series of "what ifs." She has sophisticated Social Security projection software to display visually each of your options so you can make an informed choice. It is a big decision. Do not make a mistake. There is too much money on the table—your money.

It is complicated.

14

INCOME TAX STRATEGIES

Line by Line Possibilities

The Story

THE CLOCK REFLECTED WHAT CHARLIE'S stomach was telling him, so he asked Mark if he wanted to go to lunch.

Mark navigated the Third Street traffic, keeping one eye on the road and the other on Charlie. He sensed Charlie had something on his mind.

Rosie was at their table within seconds, delivering menus, chips, and the salsa that would ignite a fire in Mark's throat, but that Charlie considered mild.

While Mark gingerly dipped one chip at a time, his eyes watering, Charlie was dipping and popping them into his mouth two, three at a time and thinking about Mark's dreams. He knew that they had shined a beacon of light on his state of apathy about his dysfunctional retirement plan. He also knew that the light had woken him up. First and foremost, he accepted the validity of Mark's Group 1 / Group 2 hypothesis. It did not take a lot of brainpower to grasp that a Group 2 person's lack of action was irresponsible.

Then, faster than you can say "chimichanga enchilada style," Rosie returned to take their orders.

"OK, guys, do you want, like, your regulars or something different?"

Charlie said, "I'll have my usual."

"Me, too, but with extra guacamole today," Mark answered, flashing his George Clooney smile.

"Come on, guys, like, try a different plate. The menu is loaded. Add some variety to life!"

Mark, without so much as a glance at the menu, said, "I'm good, Rosie."

"Me, too."

"Drinks?"

"Mineral water for me."

"Charlie, your pleasure?"

"Same for me."

"Got it. More chips?"

Mark shook his head, Charlie nodded.

Winking at Charlie, she said, "Okay, back in a Paradise jiffy with a few more chips and your food."

Charlie decided just to dive in. He started by saying, "So, Mark, Doris is, how should I put it . . . nagging me. Probably not the best choice of words. Maybe nudging me would be better. Anyhow, she's coming over to our way of thinking. She wants to learn more about what Ace is teaching you. Can you give me something new to tell her?"

"Sure—I've had more dreams. My dream two nights ago erupted like a volcano, overflowing with a blaze of illuminating statistics. Ace told me that many Americans—maybe even most—are neglecting their retirement planning. It's not on their radar. I can't give you all his statistics, but if they're true, and I don't doubt him, our country has a domestic enemy as formidable as any foreign government.

"And last night's dream made me feel good, but then it got me thinking that maybe I had missed something."

"What do you mean?"

"Ace surprised me."

Charlie raised his eyebrows and leaned forward in anticipation. "What did he say?"

"He told me that there were only two categories of

risk that could derail my plan for retirement."

"Only two? So what are they?"

"I haven't been able to recall them. I'm trying to take notes after each dream, but sometimes I get a little fuzzy trying to remember everything. You know how it is when you wake up from a dream. But they'll come back to me. I hope."

Charlie sat back, exasperated. "Mark! That would be critical information. We need to know. And I can't help but think, there must be more than two."

"Yeah, I agree. He kept repeating something else, too. He said the most important thing to do before starting the seven lessons is to figure out our character, at our roots. He meant, are we doers or chewers? Not his words, but mine."

Charlie said, "Huh?"

"You remember what I've told you about Ace saying there are two groups of people?"

"Yeah, sure."

"Okay, but here's my spin. Group 1 people are the doers. They recognize the value of preparing for life. Not living by chance, but instead living life enhanced. The Group 2 folks are the chewers. They never treat their future with the appropriate significance. They live their life by rote, much like a goat. They take each day as it comes. They say, 'Let tomorrow take care of itself.' Charlie, consider this—that kind of thinking could lead to disaster. How can tomorrow take care of itself? It can't. It's flawed thinking. They're just hiding from life . . ."

"Anyhow, the message is, conquer or be conquered. Right?

"Yes. That's Ace's constant warning."

Rosie reappeared, arms loaded with plates. "Okay, guys, like, break it up. Promised I'd be back in a Paradise jiffy, and here I am." She set the plates down and asked, "Need anything else? Mineral water?"

"We're good," said Mark, and Charlie, food already in his mouth, nodded in agreement.

"Okay, guys, like, holler."

Instantly, "the guys" were back on point.

Before Mark could say anything, Charlie, reaching for another forkful of rice and beans, confided, "I think Doris is trying to learn more about what we've been talking about without admitting she believes in your dreams. But however she approaches it, I'm on board because I know it means she wants a solution for us. When I left this morning, I asked her what she planned on doing today, and she said, 'I'm going to make a list of all our expenses.'"

Mark said, "See what I mean? There's hope, Charlie. You just need to take it one step at a time. That's what Ace says."

"Guys, like, everything taste okay?"

Charlie said, "Yeah, Rosie."

"Can I get you guys something else? More chips, salsa?"

"More water would be good," Mark responded, smiling at her.

But the big smile wasn't just for Rosie. His friend had said something that made him feel fantastic. Doris had joined the team.

Charlie prodded Mark for more. "What else has Ace taught you?"

"He has given me more food for thought. A couple of ideas. After all the statistics, he turned to, of all things, income taxes. He told me that there are ways to reduce that cost. All I know about taxes is that I pay them. Uncle Sam likes me. I'm sure he likes you, too.

"Ace wants me to hook up with an adviser who has knowledge about our tax system. He said that although it's not a fun topic, I need to have at least a basic understanding of ways to take money out of Uncle Sam's pocket and put it in mine."

Charlie, shaking his head, said, "I don't know, that

sounds like a tall order."

"Not necessarily. Ace said that if I get the right CFP®, she'll be able to give me basic information that will help me understand the ins and outs."

The Nitty-Gritty

The late U.S. Court of Appeals judge Learned Hand, who is often quoted by legal scholars as well as by the U.S. Supreme Court, said, "Anyone may so arrange his affairs that his taxes shall be as low as possible. He is not bound to choose that pattern which best pays the Treasury. Everyone does it, rich and poor alike, and all do right; for nobody owes any public duty to pay more than the law demands."

Make tax planning part of a focused method to reduce your tax bill. You may be able to move some tax dollars from the IRS's column to yours and increase your retirement savings. You are not attempting to become a tax expert. You are learning how to be a partner with your CFP® so you can construct a solid strategy to improve your prospects for life after work—that "forever vacation."

Your tax-savvy CFP® will facilitate this. However, she needs your cooperation. Give her your tax returns for the past three years. She will study that history to see what future strategies might offer fruitful opportunities.

When your CPA or Enrolled Agent prepares your tax return, she is only number crunching history. Too late for you to implement a strategy for that year. History is history. But if you track all your income and deductions during the year, your tax professional or CFP® can prepare a mock-up by shifting the numbers around to see what might generate more favorable tax results.

The reason I want you to have a grasp of these rules is so that you can see the value in the possibilities and participate as an equal partner with her.

Be aware, however, that Congress is looking at the current tax code with a goal of making major changes. No one knows how this monster project will end. On the one hand, the members of Congress may continue fighting and not accomplish anything. On the other hand, maybe they will agree on worthwhile modifications. We can only hope.

Regardless of what happens, please read what follows. You might learn ways to manipulate your tax return under the new rules. With this new knowledge, you will be better equipped to work with your CFP® and understand the new twists that might be added.

Get your tax return out. Grab a cup of coffee, a pad of paper, a writing instrument, and a highlighter. Make yourself comfortable. This is complicated, but when you take time to understand each step, it will make sense to you. It is not over your head.

I am using tax law current on January 1, 2017. The line items I explain are from the 2016 IRS Form 1040 and Schedule A.

Filing Status—Lines 1, 2, 3, 4, and 5—and Exemptions—Lines 6a, 6b, 6c, and 6d—are easy to understand. The next section is Income. You need to know the following rule. Burn it into your memory. *If you can control your income and deductions, you can control your taxes.* We will look at a variety of strategies.

Wages, Line 7, are difficult to control unless you are self-employed or employed by a corporation you control. In both of those situations, care must be taken to avoid an IRS challenge.

Lines 8a and 8b, taxable interest and tax-exempt interest, are under your control. Taxable interest and tax-exempt interest have an obvious distinction. But before you invest in either, you need to know your tax bracket. When you are in a low tax bracket, it is possible you will net a higher return from taxable fixed-income investments than from tax-exempt investments.

Lines 9a, Ordinary Dividends, and 9b, Qualified Dividends, are next. Qualified dividends receive favorable tax treatment. The rules are fairly involved and more than you want to know right now. However, this information will probably whet your appetite to learn more. If you are in a 15 percent tax bracket, there is zero tax (yes, zero) on qualified dividends. A married couple filing a joint return (MFJ) with up to $75,900 of taxable income would be taxed at 0 percent on qualified dividends. A single filer could have a taxable income of up to $37,950.

As a MFJ taxpayer using the standard deduction and personal exemptions you could have $96,700 of qualified dividends and not pay any federal income tax (single filer could have $48,350). Or it could be higher based on other factors like age and other deductions.

Line 12, Business Income, is important if you are self-employed. This is an opportunity to delay or accelerate income and time your deductions. Even a part-time business can be beneficial.

For Line 13, Capital Gain or Loss, remember this: timing is everything. Think about it—if you can time the events that result in a capital gain or loss, you can tame the taxman. The following strategies apply to your nonqualified retirement plans, not to accounts like 401(k)s or IRAs.

Real estate, stocks, mutual funds, exchange-traded funds (ETFs), business property, artwork, and so on are all capital assets. The sale of these assets will result in a capital loss or a capital gain. The losses can be used to offset gains and up to $3,000 of ordinary income. The balance of a loss not used for offset carries over to future years.

The capital gains on stocks, bonds, mutual funds, and ETFs are generally taxed at a lower rate if held for more than one year. If you hold them for less than a year, they are treated as short-term capital gains and taxed at ordinary tax rates. Long-term capital gains are taxed at 0 percent when you are in a 10 percent or 15 percent tax bracket. *No tax.* Remember, you can have taxable income up to $75,900 when filing as MFJ and still be in the 15 percent bracket ($37,950 if you are a single filer). The tax on long-term capital gains is 15 percent when you are in the 25 percent, 28 percent, 33 percent, or 35 percent bracket, which for MFJs includes income up to $470,700 (up to $418,400 if you are a single filer).

Here is a tax tip for Line 13 regarding harvesting gains and/or losses. Assume the following: You have $5,000 in unrealized long-term capital gains in one of your investments, and you are filing a MFJ return with $65,000 of taxable income. You sell the investment. Your realized capital gain when you sell will be taxed at 0 percent. You buy it back right away. You will have zero tax on the gain, and you will have increased your adjusted tax basis by $5,000. Here is an often-overlooked strategy. You have a portfolio with long-term losses of $21,450 and long-term gains of $27,150. When you net the two, you have a gain of $5,700, which will be taxed at 0 percent. No tax on $27,150 in gains. Very cool. Not sure about this? Relax—your CFP® will coordinate it with your help.

You are probably beginning to see why it is so important to keep track of all your income and deductions during the year—doing so puts you in a position of power and control. But remember, you need to meet with your CFP® to refine this tactic. Wait until the fourth quarter before finalizing a strategy. When your estimates indicate that at year's end, you will be in the 15 percent bracket (or 25 percent, if that is your target), you should look at how much you have in long-term gains and decide whether it would be profitable and tax-smart to sell. Once you have captured the gain, you can reinvest immediately in the same investment. Share values may even have dropped.

This maneuver increases your tax basis without taxation. There is no waiting period as there is when you sell at a loss. The Wash Sale Rule prevents you from taking a loss on your tax return if you repurchase the same or a similar investment within 30 days.

Line 15a records IRA withdrawals, and Line 15b reports the taxable amount. You can control IRA income until age 70½. At that age, you are required to start "required minimum distributions," or RMDs.

The 70½ rule is tricky. You must take your first RMD withdrawal before April 1 of the year following the year you reach 70½. My tax tip here is that, even though you can wait until the above date, your best bet, assuming no unusual income flows, is to take the money in the year you reach 70½. If you wait, you will have to take a withdrawal for the year you became 70½ and for the current year, which could increase your overall tax. Be aware that if you withdraw less than the correct amount, you pay a whopping penalty of 50 percent of the shortfall.

Another tax tip on this topic involves conversion of your IRA to a Roth IRA before age 70½. It is a strategy that is too complicated for these pages. But here is the tax tip. Convert a portion of your IRA to a Roth IRA before 70½ when you are in a low tax bracket. A single filer with taxable income of $30,000 could convert $7,950 to a Roth IRA and only pay 15 percent in federal tax. An MFJ filer with taxable income of $60,000 could convert $15,900 to a Roth IRA and only pay 15 percent in federal tax.

The advantage of a conversion before age 70½ is that Roth IRAs do not have RMD requirements. When you follow the Roth IRA conversion rules, you or your beneficiaries never pay income tax. Your beneficiaries do have to take RMDs, though.

Tax Alert: This approach also works after age 70½, but bear in mind, the tax rules that apply to IRAs are thorny. In the above example, before you convert any IRA to a Roth IRA, you must withdraw your RMD for that year or pay the 50 percent penalty. Do not convert your IRA to a Roth IRA without professional guidance. The rules will trip you up. You need your CFP® by your side to help you evaluate the pros and cons.

Line 17 offers opportunities with rental real estate, but this subject is very involved and beyond the scope of this book.

Line 20a records Social Security income, and you enter the taxable amount on Line 20b.

Your Social Security income claiming decision is not as simple as you might think. Your best strategy could be worth thousands of dollars in your pocket. Refer to Chapter 13.

Ready to tackle one more lucrative possibility? Schedule A — Itemized Deductions.

Line 40 on page two of IRS Form 1040 is where you record the standard deduction unless your total itemized deductions are greater than the standard deduction. The standard deduction in 2017 for a regular MFJ taxpayer is $12,700 (for a single filer it is $6,350), which is increased $1,250 each for aged and blind filers. When your actual expenses are greater, you record that total instead of the standard deduction, and you get a bigger deduction. When these two numbers are close each year, you must examine whether you should bunch your deductions or accelerate them. This strategy could save taxes and enhance your retirement bankroll.

Here is how to bunch expenses. The first category is Medical and Dental. To get a deduction in 2017, your total out-of-pocket medical and dental expenses must have exceeded 10 percent of your adjusted gross income (AGI), which is recorded on Line 37. (Miscellaneous deductions must surpass 2 percent of your AGI.)

The timing of this expense may be under your control. Instead of having knee replacement surgery in November, it might be tax-smart to delay your hospital visit until January, if possible. You may have the same control over dental work, eyeglasses, hearing aids, and other medical deductions. The trick is to bunch deductions into the next year so you can take the standard deduction for the current year and have a larger deduction the next filing period. You can do that every other year.

Note: If you are a self-employed owner of a small business,

you may be able to move the medical premium to the Adjustments to Gross Income section on page one of the tax return. That would give you the full deduction rather than the excess over 10 percent. Plus, it lowers your AGI, which is an important number affecting the calculations of much of your return.

You also can control your charitable contributions by bunching. Tell the charities you favor that you are not going to give them any money this year, but you will give them double next year.

Look at the other categories of deductions to see where this bunching strategy can be applied.

The opposite of bunching deductions is accelerating them. It can work in reverse for the current year. One example would be paying estimated tax payments to the state in December rather than waiting until January.

Caution: Do not attempt any tax savings strategies without seeking the help of a tax professional or your tax-savvy CFP®. There are caveats hiding in the bushes, for example, the Alternative Minimum Tax system, phase-out of itemized deductions and personal deductions, extra tax for Net Investment Income Tax rate of 3.8 percent, and the 0.9 percent Additional Medicare Tax. In addition, Medicare premiums are based on adjusted gross income. The higher your income the higher the premium.

At this juncture, you have more knowledge of how to maximize tax rules than you did before you picked up this book. Get professional help and learn how to benefit from the new tax law. Add your tax savings to your retirement bankroll.

Yes, it is complicated.

15

WITHDRAWALS AND ROLLOVERS

Look Before You Leap

The Story

"OKAY, I GET THE IMPORTANCE of the tax saving angle. Now what was the other idea?"

"Charlie, my friend, you're going to like the second one. I don't remember exactly what Ace called it, but he said it's a little-known strategy that may improve my overall retirement possibilities. Yours, too. However, be forewarned—it's as complicated as taxes."

"I'm listening."

"It has to do with our 401(k). I know the fees for our plan are low, although I'm not sure how much we pay. But our investment options are limited. Plus, we don't have total control. Ace said a CFP® can help me investigate the advantages and disadvantages of moving money out of my 401(k) and rolling it into a self-directed IRA. He used a special term, can't think what it was right now. He emphasized being careful and making certain I understand all aspects of the strategy. It might give us better control over our money."

Charlie said, "I know our plan has limitations, and to be honest, the cost is a mystery to me. It never crossed my mind before, but it would be smart to know."

Mark continued, "That's not the only thing that bothers me. They don't provide a well-trained expert to guide us about how to invest our money. The people at the 800 number don't talk like seasoned retirement experts. All they do is tell us what fund to use. I've asked a couple of them the same question and gotten different answers. To me, that's a red flag. My results haven't been too bad, but I don't know what I'm doing, and the helpline folks aren't a lot of help. They tell me something, and when I ask why, they give me double talk that doesn't make sense. Besides, Ace has taught me that there's more to retirement planning than just investing. I'd be a lot more confident if I had a pro to explain things better."

Charlie nodded. "I agree. Anyhow, you're right, I'm

not an expert on investing either. So what's this little-known secret? Will it help improve our results?"

"It could. Hey! I just remembered—he called it an 'in-service withdrawal.' Anyway, some 401(k) plans allow employees to take money out of their plan for any reason. You can do whatever you want with the money. But you shouldn't spend it, Ace said. If you're going to take an in-service withdrawal, the thing to do is put it in a self-directed IRA. 'Move the 401(k) to an IRA rollover,' he said. His logic is for me to get better control over my money. He wants me to be proactive and take advantage of all available options. He has said many times, I should pay a CFP® to help me."

"Are you going to do it?"

"Well, I checked with Liz in HR yesterday and found out that our plan allows this strategy. Liz said I can't do it yet, but I know it's something you can do—you should examine the possibilities to see if it's the right move."

"Why can I do it, but not you?"

"I'm not old enough. Liz said that our plan allows anyone age 59½ or older to do it. She called it something different, an 'in-service distribution,' but it means the same thing. It might be a good idea. You qualify because you're an old guy," Mark said with his flashy smile.

"Old guy? Hey, I'm only a year older than you."

"See, I'm right, you're just an old guy. You're always going to be an old guy."

"Okay, I'll talk to Liz to see what the process looks like and then check out my options. Wow, look at the time! We'd better get back to the office."

The Nitty-Gritty

The popular 401(k) Plan was written into the Internal Revenue Code (IRC) and became law in 1978. It was the beginning of the demise of the Defined Benefit Pension Plan, which is almost extinct today, other than at taxpayer-funded government agencies.

To the dismay of the American worker, this meant that the source of money to guarantee retirement income shifted from corporate America's pocket to the employee's pocket. It became the responsibility of employees to be self-reliant and set aside a percentage of earnings (elective deferral amount) to provide income for their after-work years. The deferral amount, indexed to inflation, is $18,000 for 2017. If you are over the age of 49, you can defer an additional $6,000 to 401(k) (other than SIMPLE plans), 403(b), and government 457(b) plans.

Does your company have one of these plans? If it does, you should be deferring the maximum amount each year. This is one of the best ways to set aside money to provide cash flow after you quit working.

Many companies will match a percentage of your

contribution up to a certain limit. For example, if your employer contributes an amount equal to 8 percent of your compensation, you must defer at least that percentage of earnings to qualify for the full match. If you are not saving money in your plan and your employer offers a match, you are throwing away a 100 percent gain on that part of your contribution.

Deferring money into one of these plans is tax-smart, too. The amount deferred is not included in income and will not be taxed until withdrawn, allowing tax dollars to grow until retirement.

Some employer plans include additional IRC-approved provisions that permit you to withdraw money before retirement, among them, hardship distributions and in-service withdrawals. Note, however, that their inclusion is at the employer's discretion.

When hardship distributions are included, employees can withdraw money from their plan upon the occurrence of certain triggering events, which are listed in the company's plan document. Hardship distributions are generally included in income and may be subject to an additional tax. You cannot repay hardship distributions, so such a withdrawal permanently reduces the account balance. There are serious negative restrictions and consequences associated with this kind of distribution. Be careful. It is complicated.

In-service withdrawals allow plan participants to take money out of their plan. The triggering event is attaining age 59½.

An in-service withdrawal is generally included in income to the extent it was a before-tax contribution, and it is subject to regular tax unless you roll over the proceeds to an IRA.

Taking withdrawals under any circumstance should be done only after careful consideration of all the facts. Whether it is a hardship distribution, an in-service withdrawal, or the transfer of plan funds using an IRA rollover, you must be careful. It is complicated. The following provides valuable insight.

In March 2013, the Government Accountability Office (GAO) released its results of a two-year investigation into the complicated and questionable process facing people who were changing employers or retiring and then rolling over their 401(k) to an IRA.

Much of what you are about to learn will help you if you are rolling over in-service withdrawals.

The GAO report said that in addition to being subject to inefficient rollover processes and salespeople marketing IRAs, workers separating from service may find it difficult to understand and compare all their distribution options. In some cases, the information employees receive is either too generic or lacking in detail, so they do not understand key factors necessary to make effective decisions about their savings. In other cases, the information provided is too long and technical, leaving them overwhelmed and confused.

The following will help you understand the concerns the GAO report addresses. My intent is to give you a better grasp of the issues you are facing when you withdraw money from your plan and how you might proceed toward the best possible decision.

Whether you are changing employers, retiring, or taking in-service withdrawals, you will need to make major decisions. Do yourself a favor—look before you leap. These facts will help you understand your options more clearly.

Salespeople who sell investments and insurance products will often say that an IRA rollover is your best option, without knowing all the possible benefits of your other choices. Do not take their word for it. You need to understand each of your four choices before making such an important decision. This is not rocket science, but it is unfamiliar IRS territory for the average person, including many salespeople. The IRS rulebook on IRAs, Parts A and B, is more than 100 pages. Do not expect a salesperson to have the in-depth training, know-how, and skill set necessary to assist you in making your best possible choice.

Whom then, should you ask for help? A well-qualified professional may be your best option. "Well-qualified" means a CFP® or an adviser who has training in the obscure and complicated IRS rules on IRAs, 401(k)s, 403(b)s, and other retirement accounts.

You must also recognize that whenever there is an exchange of money, there is an inherent conflict of interest. Be involved, engaged, and diligent. Reread "The Nitty-Gritty" section in Chapter 3. Remember Reagan's words: "Trust, but verify."

Caution: When evaluating which of the following choices is best for you, do not attempt to convert your 401(k) to a Roth IRA at the same time. You would be adding another layer of complexity. These are two separate decisions, so analyze them separately.

Choice number one is to leave your savings in your old 401(k). Leaving your savings in the old 401(k) might be your best choice if you are separating from service and you do not like making important life decisions. Leave the money where it is, move on, and hope for the best.

Whether you leave your savings in your old 401(k) or move it to a new 401(k), your beneficiaries in some instances may not be able to use the "Stretch IRA" option unless they are able to roll over the account to an "Inherited IRA." Under current law, this opportunity, when available, gives your beneficiaries the ability to shelter your savings from income taxes until they take withdrawals. They will be required to withdraw annually only the required minimum distribution. The annual RMDs may include taxable as well as nontaxable income, and the calculation is generally based on their life expectancy.

Employees can take loans from their 401(k) plans, but not from their IRA rollover. However, if you leave your employer without repaying the loan, it becomes taxable and you will lose all its potential tax-sheltered growth. Plus, if you are not 55 years old, you will pay a 10 percent tax penalty.

It is rare, but your old 401(k) might have some element of life insurance as part of the plan. If that is the case, tax rules state that the plan may not be rolled over to an IRA.

Whether you are changing careers, improving your employment status, starting a business, going back to school, retiring, or just living, life is complicated. Your efforts to evaluate your choices may add stress to an already stressful existence, causing you to make a hasty decision. Do not do it. Wait until you can give this possible life-changing choice your full attention.

Choice number two is to transfer your old 401(k) to your new 401(k).

If the investment options, fees, and all else are the same, you should consider this choice, as your account information will be more accessible. You will need to double-check the menu of investments. Usually, the offerings are varied, but in most 401(k) plans, investment options are limited. Make certain that the available selections meet your needs.

Caution: In the future, you may want access to the money you roll into your new 401(k), but the plan may restrict the amount you can withdraw or not allow you to withdraw any of the funds. Ask in advance if there are any restrictions on withdrawals of money rolled in from another plan. Make certain you are not prevented from making withdrawals if that option is important to you.

Choice number three is to take a lump sum distribution.

Withdrawals from a 401(k) before you reach age 55 incur a 10 percent tax penalty, in addition to your regular tax. This tax applies to the amount received that you must include in income.

This choice is an option, but a dangerous one. Do not choose it without careful consideration and some deep soul-searching. Forget about toys or personal pleasures you could enjoy now. Think instead about how much your savings might grow in the years ahead and the toys and pleasures you will be able to enjoy when you retire. You will need income then, too.

Taking a lump sum distribution will trigger income taxes, both federal and state. As a precaution, the law requires your company to withhold 20 percent of the distribution, which it sends to the IRS to make collection of the tax easier.

If you were born before 1936, you or your beneficiaries may be able to elect special ten-year averaging. Most readers are too young to be eligible for this possible tax reporting option. However, if you qualify, you will need professional guidance from a tax professional or a qualified CFP® who understands this area of the tax code.

If you elect the lump sum distribution and then change your mind within 60 days of receiving your savings, you generally may still roll it into an IRA. This is what the tax code describes as a 60-day rollover. The 60-day rollover is not recommended because (1) you only have 60 days from the date you receive the money to complete the rollover (time flies); and (2) to roll over the full amount eligible, you must reach into your pocket for the 20 percent of the distribution that your employer sent to the IRS. You will be able to get that 20 percent back from the IRS when you file your tax return the following year.

Caution: Based on a 2014 tax court ruling, Alvan L. Bobrow v. Commissioner, your ability to use the 60-day rollover option will not be available if you completed a 60-day rollover in the previous 12 months.

It is possible your future tax rate will be higher than now. If so, how much higher? That question is impossible to answer. If that possibility exists, then maybe taking a cash distribution now and paying a lower tax would make more sense.

Do not take a lump sum distribution if you want to continue to invest your money for your retirement because you will lose the tax-sheltered umbrella inherent in a 401(k) and in an IRA rollover.

There are two exceptions to the above.

First, if your old 401(k) has highly appreciated company stock, you may be eligible for preferential tax treatment on that stock. The IRC refers to it as net unrealized appreciation, or NUA. This is a little-known way to minimize income taxes on company stock held in a 401(k). There are strict rules, so if you are interested in taking advantage of this favorable tax treatment, proceed with care, and you must get the help of a tax or CFP® professional who has specialized knowledge about this subject. It is complicated.

Second, if you have a life-threatening medical condition and are not responsible to a spouse, children, grandchildren, or others, then get to work on your bucket list. Take the money. Pay the tax and possible penalty. Have fun. Enjoy the rest of your life.

Generally, however, a cash distribution is very dangerous for most people. Do not forget about the 10 percent early withdrawal excise tax penalty. If you elect the lump sum distribution option, you might have to pay this extra tax. To calculate the tax, take the total sum of the account value distributed that you must include in income and multiply it by 10 percent. If the amount you must include in income is $100,000, you will have to pay Uncle Sam not only your regular income tax, but also a $10,000 tax penalty.

Your overall tax may also increase because of a loss of or reductions in personal exemptions and itemized deductions. You may also become subject to the alternative minimum tax, and if you are on Medicare, your premiums may increase. Know what you are doing. Maybe delayed gratification should be your mantra instead of a new Corvette.

Choice number four is to transfer your old 401(k) to an IRA rollover, often referred to as a self-directed IRA.

There are no income taxes due when you transfer your 401(k) savings to an IRA rollover. You should use a trustee-to-trustee transfer when moving your retirement savings from one "custodian" to another, instead of the 60-day rollover.

(Remember what you learned above about the tax court ruling on the 60-day rollover rule.)

Do *not* automatically roll over your old 401(k) to an IRA that is with your plan's administrator or service provider. Consider them, but only after you have decided that an IRA rollover is your best choice. Then put them in the mix with everyone else. Be engaged—avoid simply taking the path of least resistance.

Withdrawals from a 401(k) after attaining age 55 are not subject to the 10 percent excise tax penalty. But note that if you elect an IRA rollover, you must wait until age 59½.

There are three exceptions:

Distributions before age 59½ that are for your qualified higher education expenses are taxable, but penalty-free.

Distributions before age 59½ for medical insurance premiums are taxable, but penalty-free if you are unemployed.

Distributions of up to $10,000 before age 59½ for first-time homebuyers are taxable, but penalty-free.

You may experience a higher level of control over your money when you roll your 401(k) into an IRA. Different firms provide a variety of customer services not found in 401(k) plans, and as a result the IRA rollover may offer expanded flexibility. Generally, investment selection is more extensive, and access to detailed investment data may be more to your liking. Determine your needs and then check out the resources available to you.

There are more options for generation-planning for beneficiaries when using an IRA. The way in which you designate beneficiaries is usually more detailed than in 401(k) plans. Tragedies, potentially extreme, can occur when this subject is not given the proper attention. In Chapter 21, you will find a detailed description of how to complete a beneficiary form.

Plans like 401(k) plans have both creditor and bankruptcy protection. If a guest in your home slips and falls, you may be liable and subject to a lawsuit. IRAs generally have only bankruptcy protection, not creditor protection. When all other indicators point you to an IRA rollover, with the primary downside being a lack of creditor protection, go for the IRA and purchase personal liability insurance. Umbrella liability policies are inexpensive and can cover as much as $25 million of personal liability.

Do not commingle your IRA rollover from your 401(k) with other IRAs unless you keep strict accounting. Annual contribution IRAs have limited bankruptcy protection. The Bankruptcy Abuse Prevention and Consumer Protection Act of 2005 provided bankruptcy protection on regular IRAs to a maximum of $1million. Inflation increases this amount. For 2016, it was $1,283,025.

When it comes to your serious money—and we are talking about one of your main retirement income resources, so this is extremely serious—you must make intelligent financial judgments. There is wisdom in securing the help of a trained professional, not a salesperson, not a service provider's toll-free adviser, and not a generic self-serve 401(k) website's FAQ or robot adviser. Remember the old saying "penny wise and pound foolish"? It applies here. Sure, you must personally be on guard whenever there is an exchange of money. Do not take anything for granted. Make certain you understand every aspect of the transaction, even when you hire a qualified CFP®.

If you skimp when choosing help with your financial decisions, in the end it may cost you more—a lot more—than you saved.

When salespeople have a commission at stake, they may not want to muddy the water with all the necessary details, assuming they know the details. Your task is to ask the salesperson why he is promoting a given product. Get his answers in writing—and then it is up to you to understand whether the reasons are valid and important to you. If it does not feel right, do not do it. Do something you understand.

Then we come to fees. There is no such thing as a free lunch. To be sure the world continues to spin, everybody needs money, so be on guard and ask about the fees you will be paying. Do not let anyone tell you that fees are insignificant. Over time, they become a vital component of your entire experience. Fees may include the expense ratio on investments, commissions, 12(b)1 fees, opening and closing fees, transaction fees, and more. Regardless of the choice you make, you will be paying fees. Know how much you are paying and what you will receive in exchange. You will learn more about expenses in Chapter 18.

There are advantages and disadvantages to each of the choices described in this section. Your challenge is to identify the best possible option based on your needs. And guess what? It is complicated.

16

IS CHICO JETTON ACE SORTS?

Is He as Smart?

The Story

IT STARTED OUT LIKE A normal Saturday. Mark
made his way to the kitchen. Winning the morning race
to the coffee grinder gave him dominion and control—
temporarily—over Lisa's territory. Making their
medicinal mix of antioxidants and adding his secret
ingredient was his reward. She did not know his secret
recipe, but it was her favorite coffee concoction, and she
had her own Saturday morning secret—letting him win
the race to the kitchen.

After taking a carafe of coffee up to her, he went back
downstairs to get his newspaper, thermal coffee cup in

hand.

There he sat, renewing his close relationship with his front porch rocker, sipping his brew. The birds were chirping their pleasant melodies, while a lazy breeze slipped between the leaves of the tall shade trees, all combining to play a soft morning symphony.

He opened the *San Francisco Chronicle*. Rocking comfortably, he flipped to the Sports section to see if the Giants won last night's game. Just as he spotted a winning score, he heard a horn blowing, looked up, and saw a car speeding up the street. Was that Charlie? Yes, it was. Why so fast? He needed to slow down if he was going to negotiate Mark's driveway or he'd land in the middle of the lawn. Was Charlie trying to imitate his favorite NASCAR drivers? They wouldn't drive on a residential street at that speed.

Charlie often stopped by on Saturday morning to chat and drink coffee. His arrival had never caused the neighbors to look out their windows. Today it did. His tires squealed as he swung a sharp right into the driveway.

Mark lifted halfway out of his chair. Why so fast? Had something bad happened? Could there be a problem with Doris? Did something happen to someone at work? What could be so urgent?

Charlie came to a screeching stop in a cloud of rubber smoke inches from the lawn. Mark watched as the door flew open, and Charlie bolted from the car. He raced toward the wraparound porch, waving a hand full of papers.

"Mark, Mark," shouted Charlie breathlessly.

"Charlie. What in the world? What has you firing on all eight cylinders? Let up on the throttle."

"Okay, okay, I'll gear down. I need to tell you something. Something astonishing!"

"What, Charlie? Everything okay?"

"Yeah, sure. It's amazing. I'll tell you why I raced over and why I'm so excited, but first I need some coffee. Anyhow, you're going to love what I'm going to tell you."

"Come into the kitchen. Lisa's still sleeping, so we gotta be quiet, please. Hush, okay?"

They tiptoed into the kitchen. Mark stopped to listen. Quiet. Good. No sounds coming from upstairs. Somehow Lisa had slept through the NASCAR arrival.

Mark thought, *I've never seen Charlie so excited. He sure doesn't need caffeine. He needs a tranquilizer!*

Charlie scooted past Mark to get to the pot, grabbed a mug from the cupboard, and poured.

Back on the front porch, Mark said, "Okay, Charlie,

why are you so revved up? I've never seen you like this. Did you win the Powerball?"

"I wish. Look! It's in my hand!"

"What?"

"Read this. It's a letter I got from a local financial guy. His name is Chico Jetton."

"So, what's so exciting about that? I get those letters a lot."

"Mark, look at the envelope and the letterhead. Look at what it says. Do you realize what this means?"

Mark glanced at the letter and envelope, then stopped cold. He looked stunned. His smile vanished, disbelief crossing his face. His mind went blank. Stillness cloaked his world.

"Mark, wake up. Are you with me?"

He shook himself back to reality. "Sorry. I'm, I'm stunned."

Charlie, still firing on all cylinders, said, "Maybe he's the guy in your dreams. Ace uses the ducks line a lot, right? Do you think Ace could be Chico Jetton? It says right here that he's a CFP®. He has all those ducks on the envelope and on his letterhead. His letter even has the duck line. You've often said that you thought a real person came to you at night. Mark, this might be the guy. Do you think it's possible? I mean, he has the same slogan. And look at the P.S. 'Are all your DOLLAR DUCKS in a row?'"

"Just a minute, Charlie, turn off your engine. I don't know. I just don't. You might be right. The more dreams I had, the more I hoped that Ace was a living person. Charlie, I gotta say—this letter makes me feel like something weird is going on, or maybe not 'weird' . . . maybe something *profound* is impacting my life, our lives. You're right; we need to investigate."

From out of nowhere, Lisa said, "Well, fellas, what's all the commotion about?"

Charlie was quicker than Mark. "Lisa, you have to see the letter I got. It's from a CFP® near the mall. His name is Chico Jetton. Look—here it is. See the ducks? And the slogan right there, just like in Mark's dreams? What's your take?"

Lisa studied the letter, deep in thought. She looked like a Stanford law professor examining a term paper or maybe a forensic expert scrutinizing crime scene evidence.

As she absorbed the ducks and the letter's content, she wondered if there could possibly be a connection between this person and Ace Sorts. After a few moments, she realized Mark and Charlie were waiting for an answer.

"My first impulse—this is remarkable."

"That's what I thought when I opened the envelope this morning," Charlie exclaimed. "Doris was still sleeping, so I left a note and raced over to tell you two."

Lisa said, "But, Charlie, I have to say, 'ducks in a row' is a common phrase. We can't be sure there's any connection. It's hard to believe that Ace could be a real person. I'd like to, but—"

Bubbling with anticipation, Charlie interrupted her. "Mark, what do you think? Could it be possible?"

Mark had fallen back into a trance. His face expressionless, his ever-present smile, missing. Lisa and Charlie looked intently at Mark. They wanted to see some excitement. They wanted his smile to return.

From the beginning, Mark had feared the dreams would stop. If they did, what would he do? That question had haunted him.

And now, Charlie's sudden early-morning appearance had opened a new possibility. Could Chico Jetton be Ace's replacement? That would solve Mark's problem. They needed someone to help them. He started to feel a sense of relief. *Could it be possible or was it merely a coincidence? Is there a connection? Are they the same person?*

Mark said, "Maybe."

Lisa put her hand up, palm facing out, like a traffic cop facing oncoming cars. "Okay, stop. I'm going to say something now, and I'd like you to please accept it in the spirit it's intended. We need to exercise some common sense. Forget about whether there's a connection between Ace and this other guy, ducks or no ducks. We need to change gears and focus on getting a human to help us. We'll start with the person who sent this letter."

Charlie interrupted the husband and wife duo. "There's a simple answer to this, this . . . ," he paused, brows furrowed, ". . . conundrum."

They both looked at Charlie, eyebrows raised.

"Okay, that's not my normal vocabulary, but I decided to search for a word that called attention to the real mystery we're facing."

Mark and Lisa looked at each other, then back at Charlie. Mark spoke. "So? What's the simple answer?"

Charlie said, "It's right there. Lisa's holding an invitation to get an honest retirement reality checkup. This guy says he will prepare a free analysis. We need to know if we're doing *anything* right, if we are even close to having our dollar ducks in a row. Sorry. I like the duck line a lot," he grinned. "We've gotta schedule appointments and learn what we need to do.

"Ace has given us an education. Okay, he's given you an education, and you've educated me. Anyhow, we, including Doris, are no longer novices on the subject. We've learned the first two lessons, which will help us decide if Mr. Jetton is at least as smart as Ace. The best thing to do is act on his invitation and then ask specific questions to see if his answers compare with what Ace taught us, taught you. You know what I mean? Anyhow, what do you think?"

Lisa was nodding. "Mark, I like Charlie's idea. We've already decided that we need someone. We'll get two birds with one stone. We can act on our commitment to each other and then figure out whether we should hire this Mr. . . . what's his name? Jetton? Think about this. Charlie might be right, maybe the guy is as smart as Ace. We need to do *something*. It would be a way to get started. You know, getting off the dime, instead of, well, just talking about it. What do you say?"

Beaming with excitement, Mark, his smile back, said, "Okay! We can make a list of questions and, as Charlie has suggested, learn what Mr. Jetton would say compared with what Ace has taught me."

The letter itself answered some questions Ace said to ask, questions about the firm's focus and values and about the adviser's experience and qualifications.

According to the letter, Chico Jetton Retirement's focus wasn't selling stocks and bonds. It concentrated instead on delivering comprehensive planning guidance to people who wanted help understanding the vast issues confronting those struggling to identify the demands of retirement.

And the letter outlined the firm's simple values. They were old-fashioned, hearkening back to the day when a handshake was all that was needed to seal an honest two-way relationship. First, the letter talked about trust—the heart of every positive human interaction— and second, it mentioned the missing link—knowledge of how to design a comprehensive retirement plan. The firm's specialty was helping people who wanted a sensible strategy.

The next paragraph settled a big question, about qualifications and experience. Mr. Jetton was a CERTIFIED FINANCIAL PLANNER™ professional, and he had become an independent CFP® 30 years ago.

So it looked like Chico Jetton was at least worth talking to, and his invitation was intriguing. He was offering a complimentary retirement and investment analysis, complete with reports. The reports would include an assessment as to whether their investments were diversified properly, a look at the extent of their stock market risk, a summary of the fees they were paying, and a determination as to whether their current arrangement could help them achieve their monetary goals.

Everyone knew it would be necessary to actively participate in the meeting. They would use what Ace had taught Mark about how to select a CFP®.

Turned out, Charlie's point made sense to everyone.

Lisa said, "Hold that thought until I get back with the coffee pot. Okay, fellas?"

Heading to the kitchen, she was tingling with excitement. Even though she did not want to admit it to the guys, she knew that, like them, she hoped Ace was Chico Jetton. She picked up the half-full pot, turned to go back out to the porch, then stopped. *Can it be? Is it possible? Is he Ace?*

Their early morning decision could be life changing, but it was time to embrace the day. It was pizza night at the Dolans. The usual gang would be there, Maggie and Gary, Doris and Charlie, Sally and Young Angus, Jill and Tim, and Angela and John, plus the kids and grandkids.

But first, Mark called Chico Jetton Retirement, Inc. and left a message that he and his wife would like to schedule a meeting.

Charlie went home and did the same.

* * *

While Lisa and Mark were preparing for pizza night, Mark's thoughts turned to Jill and John. Ace kept reminding him—in fact, was emphatic about it—to educate the kids about all of this. They need a plan, too.

He questioned himself. *Had he failed them? He had never even thought about coaching them on this part of their lives until his dreams had started. Sure, over the years, they'd had family meetings. But those never touched on anything about having a well-thought-out, structured life plan or why it's crucial to save money. The kids had a big advantage because they had a lot more years to plan, to get all their ducks in a row*—he smiled to himself—*that is, if they started lining them up now. He'd introduce the subject to them tonight, at the pizza party.*

Mark also harbored a deep concern for their friends Sally and Young Angus. They became part of the group nine years ago when they moved into the neighborhood. They had all started calling Angus "Young Angus" because he was 20 years younger than everyone else and had a baby face like Dick Clark—ageless. It was Young Angus who had started them all on games—during their first picnic outing, he suggested playing Two Truths and One Lie. Turned out, they all loved trying to baffle their friends. Young Angus and Sally fit in perfectly.

Mark and Young Angus quickly established a friendship that was more like that of a father and son. Young Angus told Mark that he had never known his mother and his father had died when he was a little boy, so he was raised in foster homes. He would often confide in Mark, sort of unconsciously adopting Mark as his mentor. It was because of their close relationship that Mark helped him get a middle management position with his firm.

Sally had a full-time job—a stay-at-home mom to three boys, Clarke, Clay, and Cheo.

Do they have a formal plan? Have they done any planning at all? He felt a sense of responsibility. He would talk with them, too, but not tonight.

Lisa said, "Mark, I can tell you have something up your sleeve for this evening's date night. Are you going to talk about your dreams?"

"Yes, I am. Of course, Charlie and Doris know my story. And I talked to Gary briefly a few days ago. We didn't go deep. No worries about my brother, though. He's the consummate planner. He has this subject dialed in. You can count on that.

"However, I think the kids and Sally and Young

Angus are different. I want them to know what my dreams have taught me. They're much younger, and like us, probably don't know how to get a plan together. We'll see. I'll react based on their level of interest . . . or lack of it."

Lisa said, "I'm not sure you should bring it up. It's not a topic people usually talk about with others."

"I have a strategy. I won't ask specific questions. I'll just explain my dreams like I did with Charlie. My story resonated with him. Maybe it will with them. I won't make it a big deal. I'll tell them what happened this morning, and what the Hatchers and we have decided to do. That's it. Don't worry," he said, giving her a wink.

Shortly after 5:00 p.m., everyone started arriving. Gary and Maggie were the first to ring the doorbell.

"Anybody home?" called out Maggie as she opened the front door.

"Yeah," Mark yelled back. "We're in the kitchen."

"Hi, guys," Gary said. "I brought wine and mixed nuts. How's everyone?"

Lisa said, "We're good. You two okay?"

"You bet, Lisa. Give me a big hug."

"Yoo-hoo! Anybody home?" the group at the front door said in unison.

"Yeah, we're in here," yelled Mark.

"The important people just arrived," said Charlie as he, Doris, Jill, Tim, Angela and John, Sally and Young Angus made their way to the kitchen with all the kids.

Mark laughed. "The important people, huh?"

Charlie smiled and said, "Hey, you're important, too."

Jill asked, "Mom, room in the fridge for the salad?"

"Yes, dear."

Grinning, Mark announced, "I have a surprise for everyone."

Charlie asked, "What kind of surprise?"

"The pizza—I'm going to grill the pizza."

Gary looked at Mark and the others without saying what he was thinking. But Maggie wasn't as reluctant.

"Did you say you're going to *grill* the pizza? On the barbecue? How in the world are you going to do that?"

Mark flashed his famous smile. "I'll show you.

The barbecued pizza made believers out of everyone—they all learned a new way to have fun making the popular Italian favorite. Only Mark and Lisa knew—or at least hoped—that everyone would learn something else before the night ended.

"Listen up, everybody," Mark said, after sending the kids out back. "I have something important to tell you.

You're going to think I'm crazy, but that's okay."

He took a deep breath and jumped in. "I've been having incredible encounters with a mystical CERTIFIED FINANCIAL PLANNER™ professional in my dreams. Get this—he's teaching me how to prepare for retirement. I know this topic is personal, and I don't want to pry into your business, but I really want to tell you what I've learned. Please keep an open mind."

Mark started from the beginning, articulating his newfound knowledge with easy-to-understand detail. Lisa watched and thought he might actually be channeling Ace. He sounded like an expert teaching adult education. She was bursting with pride.

After 45 minutes, Mark said, "Okay, that's it. What do you think?"

Gary laughed, "Nobody thinks you're crazy. I'd be willing to bet that the way you explained your dreams has lit a flame of excitement in all of us. Everything you said makes sense. You didn't give me all those facts last week. You know, I've had a CFP® for 25 years, but she told me she's retiring at the end of the year. Maggie and I should check out the guy you got the letter from. Do you mind?"

Mark said, "I'm not sure he's the right guy yet. I'll let you know after we meet with him."

17

PLANNING REQUIRES A PROCESS

The System

The Story

THE JOY OF PLANNING A well-conceived future arouses inner power and strength. Dreaming excites the imagination and stimulates the creative juices. Mark and Lisa had experienced the thrill of increased confidence when they worked through the first two lessons. But Ace had not told Mark what comes next, and they were uncertain about how to proceed. The visit to Mr. Jetton's office was on the calendar. Would he know? Their expectations were high, and anticipation increased their excitement.

Ace had taught Mark safety measures most people

never learn. He wanted to learn more. He wanted the flow of information to continue, but he was ready for a real person. He was hoping that Mr. Jetton would be Ace's replacement. Not a dream. Not a fantasy. Not a robot. A human being. A face. A smile. Someone with emotion, compassion, understanding, and a beating heart. A knowledgeable professional.

Mark wondered how Mr. Jetton would compare with the profile Ace had given him. *His letter said he was an independent CFP®, not under the control of a big corporate wirehouse.* He thought about the other questions. *Is Mr. Jetton trustworthy? Does he possess the experience and knowledge necessary to help his clients work toward their retirement objectives?* Based on the letter, Mark decided he had those attributes, *but does he have a thorough knowledge of the tax rules on IRAs and other retirement plans, enough to assist clients with their choices? Does he have a grasp of how taxes will affect their overall planning? Are his clients like Lisa and him? How many clients does he have? Does he follow a systematic procedure to determine whether they have saved enough money to live a secure financial life in retirement? Is Mr. Jetton empathetic—does he have an emotional side that helps him understand his clients? Does he prepare a written report that addresses all aspects of their financial life, including retirement cash-flow projections, or does he only sell investments and provide an off-the-shelf boilerplate document disguised as a personal retirement plan? And then the big question: Will they click?*

It would be three weeks before he would have his answers. Same with Charlie and Doris—their appointment with Mr. Jetton was later that same week. Everyone had a heightened sense of anticipation. They wanted to see whether he resembled the mystical Ace Sorts. But more important, they were ready to establish a plan with the help of an expert. Could Mr. Jetton fill Ace's shoes?

Three days after scheduling their meeting with Mr. Jetton, they received a large envelope from his office. It contained a confirmation letter with the time and date of their visit, some questionnaires, and educational articles.

One document had "Urgent" stamped at the top with a message to return as soon as possible, prior to their meeting. It would provide a snapshot of their financial state, details of their current strategy, and the planning concerns that kept them awake at night. Their answers would be the source material Mr. Jetton would use to prepare their meeting agenda.

* * *

Mark loved his coffee, loved to prepare it, loved the aroma from the moment he opened the canister until he could see the bottom of the pot. Today he decided no French press. Today he would make it Little Grandma's way. One scoop for each cup, an extra one for the pot, and his hush-hush ingredient, a pinch of salt. She had taught him this special trick when he was too young to enjoy the pleasure. He had never forgotten it.

Usually on his day off, Mark liked to sleep a little later. This day was different. He was eager to get started on the papers Mr. Jetton had sent. A special feeling was coursing through him. A remarkable sensation. A marvelous buzz pulsating through his body. He'd had this feeling only once before. He was 12 years old. He had received an unexpected present—his first bike. A brand-new racer with three gears and handlebar brakes. The silver paint sparkled like the reflective coating on a Flash Gordon rocket ship. That day, he flew like the wind, alone with his thoughts and his imagination. A thrilling new life experience, an amazing feeling—a wonderful sensation he would never forget.

He could feel that same excitement bubbling deep inside. Identical to the buzz of that long-ago joy. It pounded with noticeable force through his body. Today was the beginning of a new kind of ride. One that would capture the essence of freedom—of life. A ride that would last forever.

With heart-hammering urgency, Mark sat at the kitchen table, where he had placed his cell phone, some paper, a pen, a highlighter, investment and bank statements, and the articles, documents, and questionnaires sent by Mr. Jetton that needed answers.

Mark had always believed that an unanswered question was the same as a cone without a scoop of ice cream. Obvious possibilities, but unfinished.

Suddenly, it struck him that each year, the minute he and Lisa started to plan their vacation, questions got the ball rolling. Imagine that—they decided when, where, why, how long, and what would it cost by asking questions. Out of the blue, he felt a little ashamed to realize that they had spent more time planning their summer vacations than preparing for retirement. Then it had dawned on him that if he got organized properly, life after work could be one huge, fabulous vacation.

The idea of getting his whole life arranged reminded him of Gary. He admired and respected his brother above anyone. He ran his life with control and focused intent; he was smarter and had achieved greater success than anyone else Mark knew. Gary could be a Group 1 poster boy. He had mastered strict organizational skills. Perfect planning powered his life. He managed his money with the same commitment and had the resources to retire the same year that Donna passed away after a four-year battle with breast cancer. They had been married 28 years.

Looking back, Mark realized he could have saved like Gary. He knew he had squandered the opportunity to accumulate more money, but that was water under the bridge.

His thoughts reminded him that he must discuss this subject in greater detail with Jill and John and, of course, with Sally and Young Angus. He didn't want them to make the same mistake he had. They needed to save their money.

Mark picked up the cover letter that came with the package Mr. Jetton had sent.

Dear Mr. & Mrs. Dolan,

Are you retired or planning to retire? This is a time when you must look at your life differently so that you can see it more clearly. Your goal is a greater depth of awareness and understanding of what you want from life. Not a single picture, but a series of pictures. Will they all be beautiful scenes? The majority will, but not all. Good times as well as bad lie ahead. Smart preparation will help maximize the good and minimize the bad.

Have you made assumptions based on incomplete or inaccurate information? Know this—your behavior is governed by your assumptions. If you have false assumptions, what happens to your behavior? More important, what happens to your results? You may make mistakes that might have been avoided if you had accurate data.

There are times when highly trained professionals can provide better answers. This is one of those times.

The letter's message made sense to Mark. He reread it, and then he read the article titled "Professional Principals and Credentials."

Professional Principles

Chico Jetton Retirement, Inc. is committed to:
Serving you with honor and trust;
Providing a personalized, holistic strategy for retirement;
Protecting your confidential information;
Delivering real-time data access, 24/7;
Maximizing the planning power of technology.

Professional Credentials
CERTIFIED FINANCIAL PLANNER ™

Issued by: Certified Financial Planner Board of Standards

CERTIFIED FINANCIAL PLANNER™ professionals can be an essential resource in arranging all aspects of your financial security. These specialists are held to rigorous ethical standards. They understand the changing financial climate. The CFP Board's *Standards of Professional Conduct* require CERTIFIED FINANCIAL PLANNER™ professionals to hold your interests above their own.

Required Continuing Education Hours

30 Continuing Education hours, including two hours from a CFP Board–approved program on the CFP Board's Code of Ethics and Professional Responsibility and/or Financial Planning Practice Standards, are required every two-year license term.

Enrolled Agent

Issued by: U.S. Department of the Treasury

An Enrolled Agent has earned the privilege of representing taxpayers before the Internal Revenue Service. Enrolled Agents, like attorneys and certified public accountants, are generally unrestricted as to the taxpayers they can represent, the tax matters they can handle, and the IRS offices before which they can represent clients.

<u>Required Continuing Education Hours for Enrolled Agents</u>

Generally, Enrolled Agents must obtain 72 hours of continuing education (CE) per enrollment cycle (every three years). In addition, they must also obtain 16 hours of CE (including two hours of ethics or professional conduct CE) each enrollment year.

Mark remembered Ace telling him that their CFP® didn't have to be an Enrolled Agent, but she must have a knowledge base that included being able to read and understand IRS Form 1040 and fundamental tax strategies, and she must have detailed knowledge of the IRS rules on IRAs and other retirement accounts.

Mark poured more coffee and moved on to the next piece of Mr. Jetton's package. It was titled "Steps Necessary to Plan Your Retirement." The first step included a description of, amazingly, Ace's DNA topic. It was an exact copy. *No way. It's not possible. Is it?* He nearly dropped his coffee.

Wow! This was more than he could believe. His excitement was boiling over. He jumped up to tell Lisa, then his cell started vibrating across the table. He saw Charlie's name flashing. What timing!

"Hello, Charlie."

"You're not going to believe what I'm about to tell you."

"Yes, I will. I just, *just* this minute read it."

"Doesn't it blow your mind? Mr. Jetton *must* be Ace Sorts. He's *gotta* be. I read through his package. He described what Ace had been teaching you. He even explained the DNA thing that you told me about. I mean, this is crazy. Anyhow, what's your take?"

"Charlie, I can't tell you. I'm literally shaking with disbelief—and excitement!"

As soon as Mark got off the phone, he went upstairs to wake Lisa. She was already up, brushing her hair.

"Honey, I have something extraordinary to tell you."

"What?"

"Just don't laugh. Okay? Remember I told you about my dream when Ace explained his DNA concept? Remember?"

"Yeah, I do. Well, I don't remember exactly what it was, but I remember it wasn't the normal DNA."

"Get this. I read through the package that Mr. Jetton sent, and he has Ace's DNA example. The whole thing. It's amazing!"

"You're kidding!" But then she reined in her
enthusiasm. "Hold your horses. I agree, it's interesting,
but I'm sure it's nothing more than a coincidence."

"Yeah, maybe. But Evelyn never talked about any
DNA stuff. I think we've found our guy. I betcha he's
Ace."

Mark continued, excitement pouring out of him.
"There must be a connection. You know, supernatural?
Don't you think? Get this, Charlie called—he even
picked up on it. He thinks Mr. Jetton and Ace are the
same. I wonder if his physical features resemble Ace
. . ."

"Wait just a minute, you've never described him to
me. You actually see him? Not just hear him?" asked
Lisa. "What does he look like?"

"Yeah, it's like being at the movies. I see him clearly.
He's average-looking, an older guy with gray hair. Tall,
fit, with a lot of energy. He's like a teacher. You know,
sincere, intelligent. He talks with controlled enthusiasm,
very matter-of-fact when he gives instructions. His
words resonate with conviction. Each message just oozes
with an abundance of common sense and a richness
saturated with raw financial knowledge," he enthused.
"Sorry, I know I'm going a little overboard, but he's so
life-like. I mean, I know it's an illusory experience, a

dream. Still, he's so genuine, authentic. I can't wait to meet Mr. Jetton."

"You'll meet him soon enough. Now let me finish."

He turned to head back downstairs and get back to the papers.

"Wow. I wish my dreams were as vivid," she said to his back. "I'll be down when I get myself put together."

She continued brushing her hair. With each stroke her thoughts went from *it's impossible* to *could it be?* Then she laughed out loud.

Her mind went back to Mark and his excitement. *Dissuading him would not serve any purpose. It didn't matter if he thought Ace and Mr. Jetton lived in the same body, didn't matter at all. In fact, it could be positive. Could provide added stimulation. And more important, they're finally moving in the right direction.*

Mark returned to the kitchen. Although it seemed Lisa had dismissed him, he knew better. He knew she'd want to know what he was finding in the package Mr. Jetton had sent them. He read everything again. The 12-year-old Mark's excitement continued pounding through his body. He knew the true reason he was excited. It was the same reason Lisa, Charlie and Doris were excited. They had at last decided to do something positive, scheduling a meeting with a CFP®. A real person. Still, he couldn't ignore the possibility of a connection between Ace and Mr. Jetton.

Lisa appeared. "Well, I'm presentable."

"You're beyond presentable. You're super beautiful."

"Okay, enough," she laughed. "Let me see. No, wait, read it to me while I prepare breakfast."

As Lisa maneuvered around the kitchen, she focused intently on Mark's words, and she got a complete account of Mr. Jetton's services.

"Mark, his message describes a serious professional, dedicated to helping his clients. You agree?"

"Yeah. I like his professional principles. His credentials are what Ace said we needed. The brochure that describes his seven step L.I.F.E. Formula retirement planning system may be what we need to get our dollar ducks in a row. Okay, I know what you're going to say, but the duck metaphor really is symbolic of what we have to do."

Lisa said, "I agree."

"Honey, after reading the material twice, I've decided that we need Mr. Jetton more than he needs us."

"Well, that's a positive statement, because if he needed us, we would have an appointment with the wrong person."

"Good point. Get this—when you go through his

package, you'll see that he wants us to show him all our financial papers, living trust, will, our beneficiary forms, too. He also wants to see the deed to our home and other stuff. Do you think we should? Are you comfortable with that?"

Lisa paused to think, then said, "Yes. Of course. If we didn't do that, it would be like going to the doctor and not explaining where it hurts. Besides, we're not meeting with him to have a tea party. You said that you're impressed with his services. Our purpose is to get help. You also said that we need him more than he needs us. Based on that, we must cooperate, do what he has requested, or we'd be wasting our time. Make sense?"

"I love you, honey."

18

FEES, FEES AND MORE FEES

A Look Under the Hood

The Story

MR. JETTON BEGAN HIS AFFILIATION with his broker/dealer firm in 1993, long before registered representatives started associating with independent corporations in large numbers. He based his decision on three primary factors. First, the firm had pledged never to offer company-created investment products, which eliminated a significant conflict of interest. Second, the firm offered a no-commission, fee-only investment option, eliminating another significant conflict of interest. These two major factors helped to put the client and the CFP® on the same side of the table. The third factor was the skilled support professionals associated with the broker/dealer.

Sherrie, Chico Jetton Retirement, Inc.'s operations manager, arrived by 9:00 a.m. each morning. She would get the coffee started and then place a welcome sign on her desk to greet Mr. Jetton's 10:15 a.m. client. She knew her assistant, Denise, would have prepared the quarterly L.I.F.E. Formula reports for all clients scheduled for that day. The reports were needed to complete the progress and forecasting reviews. Before the arrival of each client, Sherrie would place the client's reports on Mr. Jetton's desk, and on top of the reports, she would place beneficiary forms linked to each retirement account and insurance contract as well as the talking points agenda that Mr. Jetton had prepared. Then she would make sure a note pad, pen, and financial calculator were at hand. If it was an annual review, she would include the client's living trust and related documents, with a verification form to record whether the client wanted her or his attorney to make changes.

Sherrie's other duties included scheduling client visits, expediting cash payouts to clients, assisting in processing paperwork for the IRS required minimum distributions from retirement plans, accounting/bookkeeping, reviewing clients' buy and sell trades, and backing up Denise.

Denise also scheduled client visits, plus she opened new accounts, routed clients' investment changes, prepared portfolio strategy review reports, processed all snail mail and email to clients, scanned and uploaded all client documents to the data management system, transmitted clients' deposits, submitted and finalized all items that had been sent to the advertising compliance department, put a second set of eyes on RMD payouts, helped clients navigate their Life Management Logic web portal, and, of course, backed up Sherrie.

A large portion of the firm's client base came from referrals. Clients, accountants, and attorneys within a 50-mile radius of the office often referred prospects. In addition, the firm regularly mailed a promotional package to potential clients that offered a no-cost, no-obligation, objective analysis of their investment and retirement plan. This was the mailing that Charlie Hatcher had received. If recipients decided they wanted a skilled professional's perspective, they would call.

Mr. Jetton gave value to all who contacted him, including those that he or they decided wouldn't be a good fit. The selection process included a thorough evaluation of all relevant aspects of a possible relationship. He focused first on the people, their personalities, and their motivation. Did they have a sincere demeanor? Did they need his help? Were they ready to participate in the process?

After arranging a potential client's visit, the staff would send an introductory package with questionnaires and other information. A sticky-note asked that all questions be answered. It clearly stated that all information would be treated as confidential and would not be shared with anyone outside the firm.

After three decades, Mr. Jetton had learned that not answering all the questions indicated a potential conflict. Those who did were probably people who had trust, were sincere about their desire to plan their finances and retirement, and wanted expert help. He deemed answering the questions part of his "good fit" test. The package also included a computer link to a secure website that had an interesting method to determine how they felt about investment risk. It gave them their "risk number."

Over the years, Mr. Jetton had refined a two-stage system to evaluate a potential relationship. His procedure would deliver both to the prospect and to him the evidence each needed to determine whether a good-fit relationship appeared possible.

During the different evaluation stages, Mr. Jetton would measure prospects' motivation, commitment, understanding of basic planning principals, level of trust, and whether they had positive or negative thoughts about their future.

Stage one was the assessment visit. It enabled strangers to get to know each other. Prospects would ask questions to learn if Mr. Jetton measured up. Mr. Jetton would probe as well, then he would study the prospects' answers and intentions to make a basic judgment. Were they committed to organizing their life? Did they want and need his help?

Stage two provided prospects with substantive answers to major questions about their current arrangement. It included a number of reports: (1) a study of all investments, before-tax as well as after-tax; (2) a determination of the portfolio's exposure to risk; (3) a summary of the total cost, including hidden fees; (4) a volatility stress test; and (5) a determination as to whether asset alignment had the potential to provide needed cash flow during retirement.

The prospects could see where they stood, what their costs were, whether the asset allocation matched their ability to accept risk, and how the portfolio might have behaved during certain past market ups and downs.

Stage two also included a rough cash-flow projection to reveal whether their money had the potential to last until age 105.

At the end of the second stage, Mr. Jetton would offer his professional opinion by giving his potential clients one of three observations: (1) the asset alignment looked good, no need to do anything different; (2) the investments needed some tweaking; or (3) a major reorganization must be considered. Whenever he recommended the latter, he would explain why as well as what the change should look like.

After all the pieces of this important analysis had been covered, Mr. Jetton and the prospects would have a heart-to-heart conversation. Did they feel they had a good fit? Did they want to work together?

The Nitty-Gritty

When you ask someone for the time, do you need to know what makes a digital clock work? Do you need to know whether the power supply is AC or DC? Do you need to know how Boolean logic and electronic gates work? Or what TTL chips and breadboards do? No, you don't. All you need to know is the time.

When it comes to your money, do you need to know what makes your investments work? Yes! You do! You cannot put your head in the sand and delegate this part of your life to someone else. It is too important. You must understand the recommendations your CFP® is making, then stamp them approved or rejected. Her job is to exercise professional judgment and target the best course of action to help achieve your goals. If you like it, stamp it "approved," but if not, "rejected"—and then examine other options.

Do you know your investment risk category? It is imperative you do. It determines your portfolio's percentage of stocks and fixed income (cash and bonds). You know that diversification is necessary. It is the simple "don't put all your eggs in one basket" rule. Everybody understands that, but surprisingly, many ignore it. Your CFP® will give you certain questions to answer so she can help you identify how you feel about risk from both an emotional perspective and what you can tolerate financially. What is acceptable to you? You may be able to accept a high-risk investment emotionally, but not be able to afford the potential loss or vice-versa.

There are five profiles. Your CFP® will quiz you to determine how much risk you feel is appropriate. The result will dictate the stock and fixed-income percentages of your portfolio.

Some CFP®s will walk you through a questionnaire or an online program to help confirm your risk classification. You should know that this process, whether a multiple-choice questionnaire or online questions, is an art, not a science.

The variations in the makeup of a portfolio goes deeper than having a lot of different investment baskets—mutual funds, stocks, bonds or exchange traded funds. There must be a specific reason for each investment in an account. All your accounts (IRA, Roth IRA, 401(k), 403(b), etc.) should be consistent with the same allocation of stock and fixed income. They must mirror each other unless there are extenuating circumstances. If you are a "growth with income" investor, you should have 60 percent of the total of each account invested in stock and 40 percent invested in cash and bonds. You can use individual stocks, bonds, mutual funds, ETFs, or a combination.

You do not pay commissions when your CFP® acts as a fiduciary, you pay fees. You need to know the fee language before you can understand what you are paying. A common annual management fee is 1 to 2 percent of invested assets. However, there are other fees, and when they are less than 1 percent, they are called basis point(s) or bp(s) (pronounced as "bip" or "bips"). One bp equals .01 percent. Think of one bp as a penny—just as 100 pennies equal one dollar, 100 bps equal one percentage point.

The annual management fee is shared by the adviser and the broker/dealer. You need to know your total cost and the deliverables you receive in return. Is it a fair exchange? Services vary and can be vastly different from one CFP® to another. Perform your due diligence to determine whether the value received is equal to or greater than your cost.

A charge you do not see on your statements or in the firm's fee schedule is an "expense ratio." This is the mutual fund manager's fee. As an example, it might have an annual management fee of 24 bps (0.24%), another fee of 15 bps (0.15%), and a service 12(b)1 fee of 24 bps (0.24%), for a total fee of 66 bps (0.66%), or two-thirds of 1 percent.

Investing money is complex. You must understand certain principles before you can make intelligent investment decisions. The following explores two important concepts.

The first is the difference between growth and value investments. Everyone invests with the expectation that the investment will grow. Think of growth and value as two different investment *styles*.

A growth stock uses its profits to expand operations. These companies usually do not pay dividends to stockholders. People invest in these corporations because they believe its price per share will rise, increasing their profit potential when they sell their shares.

A value stock has completed the growth process and pays part of its profits to stockholders in the form of dividends. There are times when these enterprises are out of favor with investors. However, bad news about them is not always valid. When there is bad news about a company's stock, the stock share price can plunge below its "intrinsic" value, the book value (assets minus liabilities) divided by the number of shares outstanding. Some people will invest only in value stocks, arguing that they are less risky.

The second concept I would like you to understand is the difference between active and passive investing. Think of them as two different types of *investment management*.

Mutual funds utilize active management, and is the traditional—and predominant—investment strategy. Women and men around a table try to outperform a targeted benchmark, like the S&P 500. Some of the time they are right. Regardless, they get paid, on average, 100 bps, or 1 percent. Numerous studies have shown that active managers struggle to beat the market, but rarely succeed on a consistent basis. Over time, management fees can become a big drag on performance.

Passive investments are just that. Passive. There is no actual management of the investments by the fund. For example, Warren Buffett suggests you consider investing in an index fund, so instead of buying a mutual fund, you invest in an exchange-traded fund. With a single purchase of a S&P 500 Index ETF, you own a percentage of 500 companies.

Passive investments will perform in relation to their benchmark, or sector's index. Most track a stock or bond index and trade immediately, like stocks. When a mutual fund trade is entered, it is processed after the market closes.

Expense ratios are much lower on ETFs, as low as 3 bps (0.03%), or three pennies on the dollar. You can learn the expense ratios you're paying by searching online.

There is significant controversy regarding this subject. Examine online information and draw your own conclusion.

Additionally, expect to pay transaction charges, which cover the cost to buy or sell an investment. These are usually nominal charges ($5, give or take) per transaction, but can add up to a meaningful number.

There may be other charges, depending on your account type. Ask your CFP® for a fee schedule.

Overall cost is an important consideration, but use good judgment. Remember the axiom "penny wise and pound foolish."

Professional advisers like Mr. Jetton are compensated for their years of training, education, and the time they have invested in fine-tuning their craft. On the rare occasion that an uninformed prospect tells a professional adviser that her fees appear excessive compared with the time it takes her to do the work, she may tell this story about a famous artist:

The artist had finished his lunch at his favorite Paris street café. He was seated near a fountain, sipping chardonnay while drawing on an oversized sketchpad. A lady approached and asked if he would be kind enough to draw her portrait. He said, "Of course, it would be my pleasure." He asked her to sit on the edge of the fountain and proceeded to transfer her image to his sketch paper.

When finished, he presented it to her. She looked at her portrait and smiled with obvious approval. Unable to hide her delight, she asked enthusiastically, "How much do I owe you?"

The artist announced his fee. The lady gasped, "That much? It only took you 15 minutes."

He paused, then looked her in the eye and said, "Madam, that took my whole life."

It is complicated.

19

SAVING MONEY IS FUN!

Avoid the Retirement Crisis

The Story

TIME SEEMED TO MOVE MORE slowly for Mark than
Lisa. He was very eager to meet Mr. Jetton. Lisa had a
more relaxed wait-and-see attitude.

Sharing all their family documents, what Ace had
referred to as Personally Identifiable Information, did
give her pause. However, deep down, she understood
that Mr. Jetton could not help them unless he knew
about their entire situation and could see exactly where
they stood in relation to all the key areas detailed on the
forms. She remembered that Mr. Jetton's letter said that
they did not have to share everything with him on their

first visit, but having those documents handy would make it possible to get answers to questions that they would not have in their heads. Knowing that put her at ease, and she felt better about telling Mark that they needed to be upfront with Mr. Jetton.

Since his very first dream, Mark had a fear they would stop and leave him hanging, not knowing how to proceed, but over time, as the dreams diminished, so did his fear. He had learned a lot. This knowledge gave him increased confidence. Plus, the thought that Mr. Jetton might be able to take over for Ace gave him comfort.

Lisa was moving around the kitchen, getting breakfast ready, when she heard, "Good morning, honey."

"Well, you're up. It's about time you—"

He interrupted her, eager to tell her the news. "It's been a while, but I had another dream."

"Really? What this time?"

"It was long. Seemed like multiple messages."

"Really?"

"And last night had a different feel. It was like Ace was having a conversation with someone else."

"Strange."

"I know. He still seemed to be teaching, but not me, somebody else."

"What did he say?"

"Heavy stuff. He kept quoting all kinds of statistics. It sounded scary. Then he reminded me that there is a retirement crisis in America. Ace said people are sinking deeper and deeper into debt and ignoring the need to save for retirement."

"What were the statistics?"

"Like before, too much to remember. Then, halfway through my dream, I figured out what was going on."

"What?"

"Ace was instructing me on how to tutor Jill and John, and it's the same message I can explain to Sally and Young Angus. I need to help them understand their situation."

"Why? You told them about your dreams, but do you think they're really interested? Don't you think the kids are too young to start planning their retirement? John is what, 30 now? And Jill's only 29. And Young Angus isn't much older. They're thinking about other things."

"Yeah, the kids have a full plate all right. But Ace was firm. He said they'd better make plans now or they'll be part of the retirement crisis. Sally and Young Angus would be in the same boat."

Mark continued, "Retirement savings might be the broccoli and Brussels sprouts on their plate now, but someday they'll say that eating their vegetables back then made their retirement 'dessert' taste much better. They'll savor that forever. I bet they'll even teach their kids to do the same thing. I've gotta have a meeting with them."

Lisa said, "Well, I guess that's a good idea. I am curious to see if they adopt a mature position or brush it off as too far down the road, saying other things are more important."

"Yeah, we'll see . . ."

He switched gears. "Honey, I was thinking about everything I've learned, and then it hit me."

"What hit you?"

"If we had started this in our 30s, just maybe we could've retired already."

Lisa looked confused. "Would you even want to retire at your age? You're only 58."

"Gary retired at 56."

"Your brother has a lot more money than we do."

"But that's the point. I mean, yeah, we've saved money, but just because. We've never had a real purpose, an actual game plan. Gary did. He had a master strategy and saved his money with the help of what's-her-name, his CFP®. She showed him what he needed to do. Remember? He reminded us about it at the pizza party. She'd been helping him for over 20 years. We tried the do-it-yourself method and didn't know what we were doing and still don't.

"Thinking about what Gary's accomplished and what Ace is teaching me made me realize that we should've started a rock-solid savings rule long ago. We should've hooked up with Gary's CFP®. I don't know why we didn't. Maybe if he'd talked to us like I want to talk to the kids, we would have. There's no doubt that if we'd started saving money back then, we would have more flexibility now—maybe I could've retired, like Gary.

"Ace says that money is not the only goal; it goes deeper. The greater goal, as he put it . . . let me think, I want to get this right . . . he told me something like, your lifetime income is limited, so you must make a conscious decision to invest and enjoy, instead of an unconscious decision to spend and regret.

"It reminded me of the Will Rogers quote: 'Too many people spend money they earned ... to buy things they don't want ... to impress people that they don't like.'"

Lisa said, "I never thought about it that way."

"There's more. Ace explained that everyone decides when to spend their money, but their decision is made thinking about the present instead of the future."

"I wish you would've had your dreams 30 years ago."

"Yeah, that would've been fantastic. It's like the old saying, 'If only we knew then what we know now.' We would have a lot more money, that's for sure. But the good news is, life's not over, we still have time. But the kids have a lot more time, if they do the smart thing *now*.

"Get this. To make his point about how important it is to save our hard-earned money, Ace said, 'What if on the day you took your first breath, you received a lump sum for all the work you would do during your life.' I mean, I know that's not possible, but just to consider his point, let's say we received all the money we would ever earn on the first day of life.

"What Ace was saying is that the key principle the kids must grasp is, when will they spend their money? Ace wanted us to know—them to know—that we have a choice. The kids have a choice. Everyone has a choice! Spend now or save and invest now so we can still pay our bills when we quit working. It hit me like a grand slam home run. Honey, it's just common sense.

"His next message scored more runs. Although a curious thought, it sounded wise, and then I realized he shared an important life principle."

"Well, what?"

"He said, 'Americans spend their money each month, making others rich, and their own bank account balances look dismal.' He wants us to tell the kids to commit to putting themselves on their own payroll, to pay themselves first, before they give their hard-earned money to others. Part of each check must be set aside—saved."

Mark continued, "Let's go back to that idea. Let's say we were given a lump sum at birth. Would we spend it all before we retired? If we died the last day at work, I guess that would be okay. But remember what Ace said? That for a couple who were both aged 65, there was a better than 50 percent chance that one would live to be 90-plus. Do you see the point?"

"Mark, you're right, we really should tell the kids. But . . ."

"But what?"

"Realistically, it would be difficult for them to save. I imagine they've stretched their budgets to the max. If that's true, how can they set money aside now?"

"Honey, Ace told me to discuss an important concept with the kids. He said to ask them what they would do if they went to work and their boss said, 'The economy is struggling, and so is this company. We need to reduce expenses as much as possible, and the only choice we have is to slash our labor costs. That means reduce payroll. We're sorry, but we must either lay you off or pay you 10 percent less until we can get back to normal. It's your choice.' What do you think the kids would do? Would they take the pay cut or start a job search?"

"I don't know. I guess that somehow they would take the pay cut and make the necessary adjustments."

"Okay, so if they're willing to accept a 10 percent cut, why couldn't they reduce their spending by 10 percent and put that money to work and—"

Lisa interrupted, "Do you think we should? How would we go about asking them?"

"Yes, of course we should. There are reasons I'm having these dreams. I believe helping others is one. We'll figure out how to do it.

"Honey, at our last pizza night, Sally and Young Angus said that they wanted to learn more about what they should do."

Mark gave her one of those great smiles, saying, "We'll do it. We'll talk to them, too."

The Nitty-Gritty

The following is reprinted with permission from the National Institute on Retirement Security (NIRS).

"Retirement Security 2017: A Roadmap for Policy Makers: Americans' Views of the Retirement Crisis and Solutions," by Diane Oakley and Kelly Kenneally.

EXECUTIVE SUMMARY

The 2016 U.S. elections made two issues abundantly clear: the nation remains deeply divided from a political standpoint and many Americans are angry about their economic prospects.

This report finds that despite deep political polarization, Americans are united in their anxiety about their economic security in retirement and in their dissatisfaction with national policy makers' inaction to address the nation's retirement crisis. This anxiety comes at a time when the once stable retirement infrastructure has degraded dramatically, resulting in a national retirement crisis for middle-class Americans. Pensions for private sector workers continue to disappear under a complex regulatory environment. Social Security benefits have been cut, and Congress is said to be eyeing additional benefit reductions. A large portion of Americans lack access to, or do not participate in, workplace retirement plans. Additionally, Americans are not saving enough in their individual retirement accounts at a time when retirement income needs are increasing thanks to rising longevity and costs. Against this backdrop, the National Institute on Retirement Security (NIRS) commissioned its fifth nationwide public opinion research project. The survey is conducted on a biennial basis to monitor over time how Americans feel about their economic security in retirement and to assess their views on policies that could improve their retirement outlook.

The key research findings are as follows:

1. Across party lines, Americans are worried about economic insecurity in retirement.

Three-fourths (76 percent) of Americans are concerned

about economic conditions affecting their ability to achieve a secure retirement. For respondents that identified themselves as Democrats, the level of concern was at 78 percent compared to 76 percent for Republicans.

2. Americans in overwhelming numbers continue to believe the nation faces a retirement crisis.

Some 88 percent of Americans agree that the nation faces a retirement crisis, holding steady from 2015 (86 percent). The level of concern is high across gender, income, age and party affiliation. Importantly, more than half (55 percent) strongly agree that there is a crisis.

3. Americans regard pensions as a route to economic security in retirement, and see these retirement plans as better than 401(k) accounts.

We find that some 82 percent of Americans have a favorable view of pensions. A full 85 percent say all workers should have access to a pension plan so they can be independent and self-reliant in retirement. More than three-fourths of Americans (77 percent) say the disappearance of pensions has made it harder to achieve the American Dream. Some 71 percent of Americans say that pensions do more to help workers achieve a secure retirement as compared to 401(k) plans, and 65 percent say pensions are safer than 401(k) plans.

4. Americans say national leaders still don't understand their retirement struggle, and they remain highly supportive of state efforts to address the retirement crisis.

An overwhelming majority of Americans (85 percent) say leaders in Washington do not understand how hard it is to prepare for retirement, which held steady from 87 percent in 2015. Similarly, 86 percent say leaders in Washington need to give a higher priority to ensuring that Americans have a secure retirement. In terms of solutions, 82 percent of Americans say government should make it easier for employers to offer pensions. Americans also believe that state-sponsored retirement savings plans for workers not covered by an employer's plan are a good idea (75 percent), and 81 percent say they would consider participating in a state plan.

5. Protecting Social Security remains important to Americans.

Some 76 percent of Americans say it is a mistake to cut government spending in such a way as to reduce Social Security benefits for current retirees, up from 73 percent in 2015 and 67 percent in 2013. When it comes to benefits for future generations, 73 percent oppose cutting government spending that reduces Social Security benefits.

6. Americans strongly support pensions for public sector workers and see them as a strong recruitment and retention tool.

Americans strongly support pensions for police officers and firefighters (90 percent) and for teachers (81 percent). The research also finds that Americans overwhelmingly support retirement security for workers who face job risks, such as corrections officers (90 percent). More than half of Americans (52 percent) believe that public pension benefits levels are about right at $2,205 per month, while 37 percent say the benefits are too low. Americans overwhelmingly agree (92 percent) that pensions are a good way to recruit and retain public sector workers like teachers, police officers and firefighters.

***

The NIRS analysis is revealing. Americans are not saving enough, and they are fearful about their future. The report emphasizes a serious concern. Private pensions are almost extinct. Corporate America's shift to 401(k) plans has been extensive because it transferred funding from the corporation to the employee.

Do not count on a shift back to private pensions. Do not count on the federal government. Do not count on an inheritance from a rich uncle. No lottery winnings either. Count on yourself. *You* must do what is necessary for you to have a secure life in retirement.

How long will you live? As discussed in previous chapters, this is an important question. You have learned that you should plan to have enough money stockpiled to provide income flow to age 105. The statistics provide a guideline to help you answer the question. Regardless, if you retire at age 67, you might need money for 30 years or more. How much money will you need to last all those years?

Albert Einstein said, "Compound interest is the eighth wonder of the world. He who understands it, earns it . . . he who doesn't . . . pays it." Compound interest will help fortify your retirement lifestyle. Adopt a saving habit. Invest part of every dollar you earn. Pay yourself before you pay anyone else. Put *You* on your payroll. You are worth every dollar.

If you are not already saving and investing, do this: start setting aside 4 percent of your gross income from each paycheck. Accumulating money through a 401(k) or other qualified retirement plan may be your best option. Your savings will be invisible and tax deferred. You will not miss such a small amount. Four percent is doable. Next year, add 4.5 percent. This additional savings will be tough, but you need to exercise commitment. The next year, add 5 percent. Win the battle. At that stage, you will be paying yourself 13.5 percent per year, almost as much as you pay Uncle Sam. Continue to pay yourself first until you retire. Put Einstein's wisdom to work. The feeling is like nothing else you have experienced.

Your savings and investment strategies will help you live a more comfortable retirement. You may even be able to retire earlier. That extra dinner you put off today is a dinner you will enjoy with added pleasure tomorrow.

Plan a long life. DREAM BIG, SAVE BIG—so you can LIVE BIG.

20

THE FIRST MEETING

Examine all Factors

The Story

THE DOLANS AND THE HATCHERS were enthusiastically anticipating their visit with Mr. Jetton. They coined a phrase to symbolize their eagerness: CJ Day. All data forms, including signed beneficiary forms, monthly spending pattern information, quarterly investment statements, wills and living trust, recorded deed(s) to real property, and three years of tax returns, had been assembled.

CJ Day for the Dolans had arrived. Mark did not like being late. He input Chico Jetton Retirement's address into his cell phone's navigation app. It indicated a 53-

minute drive. Lisa knew that he would want to leave earlier than necessary in case traffic was slow.

They reached a small business park with some 30 minutes to spare. Lisa shook her head and smiled to herself—par for the course for them. Mark had spotted a coffee shop a block back that sold his favorite lemon loaf, so he circled back and turned into its parking lot.

They savored their coffee, Mark exclaiming about the lemon loaf, then got in the car and returned to their destination, a building in a modestly impressive single-level office complex. They checked the directory, saw that Chico Jetton Retirement, Inc. occupied Suite 130. They entered at precisely 10:15 a.m. The receptionist's desk had a sign that said, "Welcome Lisa and Mark Dolan."

The office manager, Sherrie, greeted them with a friendly smile and warm handshake. She invited them to be seated, then said, "Mr. Jetton will be with you shortly."

Beautiful pictures of Hawaii graced the walls, in addition to some awards, plaques, and certificates of accomplishment.

Inside of two minutes, he walked into the waiting area and extended his hand to introduce himself. He said, "Hello, I'm Chico, Chico Jetton. Please call me

Chico. It's a pleasure to meet you. I've reviewed the data forms you returned. Thank you. I would like to go over them with you, but first, follow me—I'll give you the tour."

He showed them the support staff offices and provided brief introductions. One large office had an impressive mahogany desk, chairs, a sofa, and pictures of old-time baseball pros.

Chico asked them to follow him into another room that had a round table, three comfy-looking chairs, plus one that looked like the boss's, a big-screen television on the wall, a white board, a conference telephone, and windows facing the busy street.

He asked them to take a seat and make themselves at home. Sherrie had followed quietly behind. When seated, she asked what refreshment they would like. Both said black coffee.

A talking points agenda and their completed data forms rested directly in front of Chico's chair.

Small talk filled the gap until the coffee arrived, which Sherrie delivered within a couple minutes. The exchange of pleasantries seemed to serve its purpose, relieving the initial stiffness.

Chico began with a question. "Is there anything you want to ask before we start?"

190

"Yes," Mark said. "I've been investing money for years, but recently I realized there's more to it than meets the eye. So I decided to become a recovering do-it-yourself investor. Can you give me an example that might prove why my decision was the right one?"

"Of course. You're certainly not alone in your choice. But first, may I ask you why you've made this important turn-around?

"Sure. Although I'd like to wait until I get to know you better before I give you my answer. Is that okay?"

"That's fair enough."

Lisa said, "Mark's done an adequate job investing our money. We have a broker, too, but Mark does the lion's share. Recently, we both learned there's more to it than picking a five-star mutual fund. It became clear that investing was simply part of a much bigger picture. The way that revelation came about is, well, out of the ordinary, and that's why Mark wants to delay giving you all the details."

"Again, fair enough. So, to answer your question—I could bend your ear for hours giving you examples. There's one heartbreaking and complex story, though, that resonates with everyone who wants to understand the value a professional adds.

"An anxious man called late one afternoon saying his

friend told him he needed my help. His words and tone indicated he wanted what could only be classified as an emergency appointment. Fortunately, my schedule allowed me to meet with him the next morning.

"This sweet man had come to me after he had accepted that he needed professional help with the magnitude and scope of his financial life, and that needing help wasn't an indication of weakness or lack of intelligence—just the opposite. His personal life had another layer of complication, health issues that required repeated visits with medical professionals.

"He was married to his second wife and had three children from his first marriage. The second marriage happened late in life. He had his assets, she had hers.

"He told me he'd been a successful do-it-yourself investor, but there were significant losses in his portfolio. He attempted to conceal his embarrassment, but it wasn't necessary. Even the pros lose money.

"He wanted help getting his financial life organized. We did that, meeting four or five times. We modeled his L.I.F.E. Formula retirement plan to fit his needs. It got all his financial ducks in a row. In the process, I discovered a serious and costly tax issue with his IRA. I had his CPA fix that problem.

"He wanted to divide his assets four ways, equally

between his children and his wife. My attorney reviewed his estate documents and made sure everything reflected his wishes. Everything was falling into place. He expressed his pleasure and satisfaction more than once.

"When he came in for his first quarterly review, he told me he had learned the true nature of his health problem. He said, 'I'm going to die.' The doctors gave him less than 90 days. I didn't know what to say. I was so sorry.

"Part of his plan required harvesting substantial losses over an extended time, but his deteriorating health required an abrupt change in strategy. You see, tax law cancels investment losses at death. No one gets to deduct them. It's the ultimate tax loss. The losses are gone forever.

"Letting that happen would only benefit Uncle Sam. I needed to come up with a new twist, a new plan. This man had lost tens of thousands of dollars on his stock purchases.

"Consider what would happen to most people in that situation. No one gets to use the losses when they die. Here's the reason: Let's say an investor bought $100 of stock, as her sole and separate property, and died with a $25 loss. If her child inherited the stock after she died, the child's tax basis would be its fair market value, $75, not $100. If she had gifted stock to a son or daughter before she died, the child's tax basis would be the same, $75.

"But I knew something a do-it-yourself investor wouldn't know. It's complicated, but my revised strategy distributed the dollar value of his assets equally to his wife and children, just the way he wanted, with one big exception. I calculated the value of each beneficiary's interest, and then without diminishing anyone's value, I suggested he gift the stock with most of the losses to his wife before he passed. She got her share, and the balance of his estate went to his children later. It required another meeting with the attorney to amend his living trust.

"There's a little-known section of the tax code that says when gifting an asset to a spouse, the adjusted tax basis to the donee is the same as the donor's. So if you gift separate property to your spouse while you're living, your spouse gets your adjusted tax basis. Gift the stock to anyone else and their tax basis is the lower of fair market value at the time of the gift, or the donor's lower adjusted tax basis.

"So his wife enjoyed the tax advantage of deducting the losses of more than $250,000."

Lisa said, "Sounds like you really helped her. She

must love you."

"It's kind of ironic. When he told her he was going to hire me, she asked him why he would want to pay someone to do what he had been doing for years."

Mark said, "She got her answer, didn't she?

"Yes, and she became a loyal client.

"Does that story sort of give you a sense of why working with a professional is a good idea?"

Smiling, Mark said, "Yeah, the old two heads are better than one axiom. Especially when one head knows what the other head needs to know."

"Any other questions?"

Lisa said, "I have one. You've mentioned your L.I.F.E. Formula planning system. We read your brochure, but could you give us more detail?

"Certainly. L.I.F.E. is an acronym for Live, Imagine, Focus, Enjoy. There are seven steps that I use to plan for my clients. What I've learned over the years is that people live life imagining what they want their life to include. Certain people don't go any further. They only live and imagine. But others don't stop there. They move forward and focus on the actions that must be implemented to experience what they imagined, the hard part required to make it real. The result is that they have a better chance to enjoy the experiences they imagined. It's not magic. It's something you must work at to achieve. My system helps facilitate that endeavor."

He paused. "Anything else?"

Even though Mark and Lisa had a list of questions, they looked at each other and shook their heads. They were already convinced they were with the right person.

Chico continued, "I'd like to offer you my compliments. People would rather see their dentist than their attorney, their doctor instead of their dentist, and some would prefer to go to the movies rather than meet for the first time with a CERTIFIED FINANCIAL PLANNER™ professional. But you're not at the movies—you're here. So my compliments to you.

"In a minute or two, I'd like to ask you if there is a specific concern that motivated you to meet with me. But first, with your permission, I'd like to describe my firm's specialty, the reason our family of clients decided to hire us, and our business values. Is that okay?"

Lisa said, "Yes, that would be good. We're interested in what you have to say."

"We focus our efforts on helping people who are concerned about their retirement obstacles and how to plan properly for a safe, secure retirement. No one wants to make avoidable mistakes or outlive their money. My team's planning system is designed to simplify the process. And we make it as trouble-free as possible.

"There are three key reasons our family of clients decided to hire us and commit their loyalty," he continued. "First and foremost, they know we're trustworthy and will only make recommendations that are in their best interest. Second, complexity foils execution. It encourages procrastination. The astute are aware of that and want help navigating the difficult financial issues facing them every day. They know the do-it-yourself method is saturated with dangerous and unknown consequences. And third, clients demand and we deliver professional, knowledgeable, quality service tailored to each person's individual needs.

"Everyone's situation has similarities; at the same time, each is unique. So we start with and continue to focus on what's most important to you.

"The data forms you completed and returned to me are in good order. I have created an agenda based on your answers, and I'm well prepared to discuss several topics, all focused on helping you.

"First, I need to understand your personal goals, priorities, and attitude toward risk—simply put, your hopes, dreams, and fears. Next, I want to help you make sense of the financial markets with a realistic look at what's happening out there, the good as well as the bad.

"Everything my firm does is designed to accomplish a key purpose: to lend a knowledgeable helping hand to those seeking a secure plan for and during retirement.

"Before we establish a client-adviser relationship, we provide you with an analysis of your current retirement plan and investment strategy. When we complete and review that initial report, we'll see where you stand and whether you need professional help."

The discussion and the way he presented the material resonated deeply with Lisa. She realized that the words she heard were conveying the same ideas Ace had taught Mark. She sensed Mark was thinking the same thing. Chico's message gave her reassurance that they had made a smart decision bringing all their records and being open. She felt abundantly confident. Chico was going to make a positive difference in their lives.

The Dolan's visit lasted just under two hours. It seemed impossible to have covered as much material as they did, but it was obviously a testament to Chico's professional skills. Everything fell into place.

Chico asked, "Do you have any other questions?"

Mark turned to Lisa as he answered, "No, I don't. Do you, Lisa?"

"No. I have seen and heard enough to know that we

need your help. I can speak on Mark's behalf. We both want to hire you. You do agree, don't you?" she asked Mark.

Before Mark had a chance to answer, Chico said, "Even though we've exposed several issues that need attention, I've learned after working with clients over the years, or maybe it's just because I'm an old guy, that it's better not to make impulsive decisions. A superior result can be achieved when you take a step back to contemplate everything after a cooling-off period.

"I'm excited about the idea of helping you, but I must do what I'm going to ask you to do, and that is to take some time. Evaluate precisely how I can help you. Am I competent to help you? Most important, will we be a good fit over the long haul? We both must be able to answer yes to that question.

"Waiting until I've completed and presented your analysis will give us time to evaluate each other. When that second stage is in the books, we can have a frank conversation to see if we both feel like we want to work together. I hope you agree.

"Sherrie will schedule your next visit. It will take two weeks to prepare your analysis," he said. "If you or I decide that we are not a good fit, your time will not have been wasted. You will at least have gotten answers to important questions about your financial life."

The knowledge Chico had gained over the years taught him what he needed to see in people before accepting a new relationship. He must be certain they wanted to get their financial house organized and were willing to commit to doing their share of the work. He knew trust would be the foundation forming their relationship. And then the fit—would they be a good fit?

Chico continued, "Does this procedure make sense?"

Lisa and Mark both nodded their heads.

He stood to signal the conference had finished

Lisa asked, "I suppose you're going to need us to leave these files?"

"I'll need the data forms and your monthly and quarterly statements on the investments. Also, there was something in your tax return that I want to double-check, so leave that, too. Sherrie will give you a receipt for the documents, and when I'm not working with them, they will be locked up in our file room. The custodian doesn't have a key. They'll be safe."

Chico accompanied them to Sherrie's office, and she prepared a receipt for the items left behind, then scheduled their next visit.

* * *

Lisa and Mark had decided beforehand to lunch at

their favorite bistro, which was near Chico's office. They didn't talk to each other until they were seated with menus in hand.

Lisa spoke first. "Mark, what do you think?"

"He's fantastic. Look at the issues he pointed out. We're not even clients, and he's helping us get squared up. I mean, just deducting our fees is a big deal. I didn't know we could. Why didn't Evelyn tell us to do that?"

"I don't know. I think because she's not a CFP®."

"Honey, his little demo of how we can create an actual written document about our plan through interactive participation with him is what Ace said we needed. I mean getting something concrete is major. He said, 'Get your plan in writing.'"

"Yep," said Lisa. "I liked the Life Management Logic demo, too. The ability to see everything in one place is convenient. It'll save time and make checking our account balances a piece of cake."

21

YOUR BENEFICIARY FORM

Underrated, Misunderstood

The Story

AS THEY HEADED HOME, LISA shifted to organizational mode. "Well, over the next two weeks we must review everything we've talked about, especially the issues regarding our beneficiaries and what he said about the questions with some of our documents. The incomplete beneficiary form on our 401(k) and the IRA could be a serious concern under the wrong circumstances."

"Yeah, Evelyn never said we needed to have another level of beneficiaries to back up our contingent beneficiaries. He's right—if one of the kids dies before us, and we die or become incapacitated before making the necessary changes, it would be a total mess. We need to fix that. I know Chico will if he decides we're a good fit."

"Mark, he wants us to figure out if we have the right chemistry. He also said we need to evaluate whether we got the sense that he has the professional ability to help us."

"Yeah, I get that. But honestly, there's no question in my mind."

Lisa changed the subject. "I'm glad we arranged with the Hatchers not to discuss our visit with Chico until after they meet with him."

"Yeah, they'll have an open mind and maybe a different perspective."

The Nitty-Gritty

Mr. Jetton asks prospective clients to bring certain family documents to their meeting. Beneficiary forms top the list. Why? Because it is one of the most underrated, undervalued, unappreciated, misunderstood legal forms you have signed. Sadly, the person who helped establish your account may suffer from this common deficiency and does not understand its vast importance or how it should be perfected.

Do you have a qualified retirement plan, annuity or life insurance contract? Can you find the beneficiary form you signed? This is one of your most important legal instructions, distributing mountains of money. Consider this question: Do you have your wishes spelled out correctly? Are you sure?

Read this excerpt from an email sent to me by an attorney regarding his late client's omissions when executing his beneficiary selection documents. The client was an investment broker and should have known better, but regrettably, he did not dot the i's or cross the t's before he signed each beneficiary form. His family experienced the frustration he mistakenly willed to them.

I have removed the principal's name and the names of the financial institutions.

***

You won't find much on the record about the case I mentioned because it was settled out of court. My [client], a really nice guy in his late 70s, was still working at [major wirehouse] after a long career in the securities business. He had three awful, awful children and had just married his longtime live-in girlfriend when he suddenly and unexpectedly died. (As a side note, he named [his bank] as his executor and successor trustee, but after dealing with his family for a couple weeks after his death, it refused to take either position. None of the family members were willing to front his funeral and burial expenses, so the [bank] representative did so and then had to have me intervene with the family to reimburse him.)

[Client] had a $5,000,000+ IRA (it could have been a 401(k) I suppose. I can't remember, but the legal issues would be the same either way) at [major wirehouse]. The [major wirehouse's] Beneficiary Designation Form was poorly designed, and [client] filled it out incorrectly. He named Child #1 the primary beneficiary of 1/3. He named Child #2 the contingent beneficiary of Child #1's 1/3. And he named Child #3 as the primary beneficiary of 1/3. There was no primary beneficiary named for the remaining 1/3. The Beneficiary Designation Form indicated that the default beneficiary of any undesignated portion would be the participant's surviving spouse. As you can guess, this caused very expensive litigation between Child #2 and the new widow. As a side note, [client] was supposed to name his trust as the beneficiary of a large life insurance policy he had at [major wirehouse], but he left the beneficiary form blank, causing the trust to have insufficient cash to make a large cash distribution to the widow. More fodder for litigation. As I said, [client] was a nice guy and supposedly trained by the brokerage firms he worked for on how to fill out beneficiary forms for his clients and he still totally messed up.

***

Here is another example. This was a high-profile case that made its way to the U.S. Supreme Court: *Kennedy v. Plan Administrator for DuPont Savings and Investment Plan* (No. 07-636, decided January 26, 2009).

Mr. & Mrs. Kennedy divorced in 1994. As stipulated in the divorce decree, Mrs. Kennedy waived her rights to any benefits under Mr. Kennedy's retirement accounts at his firm, E.I. DuPont de Nemours & Co, where he had worked for 34 years.

The retirement account in question was valued at $402,000 when Mr. Kennedy died. He allegedly wanted the account to go to his daughter Kari Kennedy. However, he did not execute a valid beneficiary change form. Consequently, the high court ruled that the beneficiary form on file would prevail. It gave the entire account to Mrs. Kennedy.

Regrettably, a situation that is played out with different

characters and storylines countless times across America. You must be absolutely certain that each account you have has a properly executed beneficiary selection form.

When this step is neglected or not completed correctly, the institution has default provisions that take effect. Do not use them. Complete their form, and if their form is not formatted to say what you want, you need to ask your CFP® to attach a separate page with clear instructions on how and to whom the proceeds should be distributed. Make certain the custodian will accept your written instructions. If the custodian will not, move your account to a new custodian. Also, do *not* say "per my will" in your instructions. Big mistake.

There are other key factors you should know. In community property states, qualified retirement plans require the spouse to consent to your beneficiary selection when someone other than the spouse is named. Some non-community-property states also require a spouse's consent.

Most married people select their spouse as primary beneficiary and their children as contingent beneficiaries. Adding Per Stirpes, or Right of Representation, language to the wording will distribute proceeds to the children of deceased children; from one generation to the next.

An issue that may develop when younger beneficiaries receive a lot of money is that it can confuse normal brain waves. Including a delay provision until certain ages are reached may be your best way to protect younger beneficiaries from themselves. The language to do that is tricky. Your CFP® will help with the proper wording.

In some situations, people use the Per Capita language instead of Per Stirpes, which will distribute funds to the then-living children equally rather than flowing down to the next generation. In this example, the children of a deceased child are disinherited. That would be okay if that was what you wanted.

Be alert to situations that would cause you to want or need to make a change, for example, divorce, death, name changes, marriage, birth of children and grandchildren, and a beneficiary having personal issues that would cause you to believe they would not manage the money properly.

Do this: list every insurance contract and retirement plan you own. Contact each provider and request a copy of the beneficiary form they have on file. Verify that it details your exact wishes and is stamped as accepted by the custodian.

I repeat, the beneficiary selection document must be executed with care. You cannot redo it after you die. Lean on your CFP® for help.

It is complicated.

22

COMPARE NOTES
*****

4 Heads are Better Than 2

The Story

MARK'S DREAMS AND HIS FIRST meeting with a
CFP® had taught him that there is more to the challenge
of finding a competent and compatible CFP® than
picking the closest office or flipping a coin

His gut told him his search had ended, and Lisa felt
certain, too. But . . . would Chico agree?

The Dolans and the Hatchers often had Saturday
barbecues in the Dolans' backyard. They had fun, they
laughed a lot, and they would try to top each other with
their tales. However, this Saturday would be different.
They had a mission. Both couples had had their

exploratory meetings with Chico, and they wanted to compare notes.

Charlie took control as head chef at every barbecue. He had a special skill. He knew when the meat had reached "plate perfection." He had a method—he would put different fingers together with his thumb and then press on the ball of flesh at the base of his thumb to compare its firmness with the feel of the steak. His index finger detected medium rare, middle finger, medium, ring finger, medium well, and little finger, well done. Seemed silly, but somehow Charlie's technique resulted in a perfect steak for everyone every time.

The Dolans were eager to hear about the Hatchers' visit and what they thought of Chico.

Mark heard the door open and then Doris's voice.

"You inside or out back?"

"In here," Lisa called out.

Everyone exchanged hugs while Mark served their usual beverage choices. Then they made their way to the shaded patio.

Lisa spoke first, "Okay, we can't wait to hear—please tell us your verdict on Chico."

Doris answered, "We like him a lot, but we're not sure he liked us. He said we needed to wait until he completes our reports before he'd decide if he wants us. What did he tell you?"

"He told us the same thing. Mark and I told him we were ready to get started. In a way, we already have, but whether it's going to be permanent? We'll just have to wait and see."

"First impressions are important," said Doris. "When Charlie and I walked into his office, we saw a welcome sign with our names. That hit me as being extra special. The office was top quality, wasn't it? Not *too* fancy, but more important, we connected with Chico."

The men were silent spectators, waiting to talk. Doris and Lisa were intellectually dissecting every nuance of what they remembered Chico had said about getting all their dollar ducks in a row. A Socrates quote crossed Mark's mind: "Once made equal to man, woman becomes his superior."

Doris continued, "His style impressed me. He flipped through our trust papers and found a mistake that he said should be fixed."

Lisa said, "That's interesting. What?"

"On our living trust, Charlie and I have you as our successor trustee and Mark second. But somehow our financial powers of attorney designate my brother as the attorney-in-fact. Chico asked some questions, then said it should be you and Mark on all documents."

Doris continued, "Mark, remember you told Charlie that he could take his 401(k) and move it to an IRA rollover? Chico asked Charlie some questions about whether he wanted more control over our money. He mentioned some of the same advantages of doing what Ace told you."

"You mean the in-service distributions?

"Yeah, that's it. Charlie said we should do it if Chico decides to work for us and his analysis says it's a good idea."

Lisa wanted to brag. "Listen to this—within minutes, Chico found two problems with our stuff. This is crazy. As in, not good. He looked at our investment statements and tax returns, then asked why we haven't been deducting the fees on our investment accounts. Evelyn never told us we could. We've paid her company a lot of money over the years and never deducted a dime. Chico said that Evelyn should have billed us directly instead of taking fees out of our IRA account because that way, they'd be deductible. He also said that we're not even deducting the fees for the accounts that aren't IRAs. That's Mark's fault. He didn't know we could and those don't need special billing. We're not even paying him yet, and he's saving us a pile of cash.

"Those strategies would make most of the fees deductible. He said all you have to do is exceed 2 percent of adjusted gross income to get the write-off on Schedule A, the itemized deductions form. I wonder what Evelyn will say when we have that conversation."

Mark decided to participate. "He gave us some other good advice. He explained how our beneficiary forms would distribute the funds if either or both of us died. Lisa and I are each other's beneficiary on our retirement accounts, and the kids are the contingent, but no one else. Chico said that it's necessary to have our bases covered. We should add the grandkids and something else, it was a Latin term, in case the kids die before we do, or we should direct those proceeds to our living trust. And then he told us to add a special delay provision in case the money gets down to the grandkids before they're 30. He said, 'It's unlikely the kids would die before you do, but in case, you don't want the grandkids to get all that money when they turn 18. A red Ferrari, if you know what I mean.'"

To commemorate the occasion, Mark brought out a special bottle of wine to complement the steaks, roasted potatoes, vegetables, and Doris's salad.

Charlie looked at the label. "Hey, no way! A 2008 Scarecrow cabernet sauvignon? Wow, we're definitely celebrating tonight."

Mark said, "I've been saving this gem to honor a special day. Today's the day."

Charlie said, "I guess you think Chico will agree to help you."

"Yes, I do. Well, I sure hope he does.

"Let's discuss the link between Chico and Ace. Ace talked about his Total Retirement Solution. It had seven lessons. Chico calls his planning system the L.I.F.E. Formula, and his process refers to seven steps, not lessons, but there are seven of them. It's the same thing. There're so many similarities."

Charlie said, "No kidding. You're going to love this, Mark. Remember when you told me Ace said there were only two risks?"

"Yeah. That's the only thing he has said that made me skeptical."

"I'll restore your faith. Chico said the same thing."

"He did? Did he say what they were?"

"Yeah. You're going to laugh. He said, 'There are only two kinds of risk. The obvious and the not-so-obvious.'"

Mark grinned. "These two guys could be the same person—"

Doris interrupted with a half-hearted smile, "I've

come to an obvious conclusion. Rational judgment dictates only one supposition when reasonable people exercise intellectual review of the facts. Forgive me everyone, but no, there's no connection. It's a coincidence. Ace is not Chico. Plain and simple. Let's move on."

Lisa, laughing, said, "I agree."

While the women continued their conversation, Mark started clearing the table. He took everything into the house. Charlie decommissioned the barbecue and enjoyed his last sip of Scarecrow.

23

PRESENT ANALYSIS

Good Fit Decision

The Story

MARK ARRANGED A PERSONAL DAY away from the office so he and Lisa could meet with Chico to get his retirement and investment analysis reports. They were eager to learn whether their money had been positioned properly, how much they were paying in fees, and—a key question—how long their savings would last after they retired.

After some small talk, Chico started by saying, "Imagine you are in a boat. Call it the financial boat of life. You're the captain, and I'm the rudder. I will guide you through rough waters, but first you must tell me where you want to go. Before you can tell me where to guide you, you need to know where you're starting from—your current longitude and latitude. That's what we'll cover today."

Lisa said, "Sounds good. We're all ears."

Chico continued, "Investing money is serious business. If you think it's as easy as picking the latest and greatest mutual funds, think again. A five-star fund today might be a two-star fund tomorrow. There's more to engineering the elements of a successful retirement than merely investing money. There's much more under the hood. It's that age-old problem—you don't know what you don't know. That's when you turn to someone who knows what you need to know. I can help you do that.

"You must have a complete understanding of precise principles and their complexities before you can make intelligent decisions about your future. I have a rule. Never nod your head yes when I ask you, 'Does that makes sense?' if it doesn't. Make me explain it differently, with clearer examples.

"The online risk questionnaire you completed tells me you're in a midlevel risk classification. You're concerned about investment losses, but still want to grow your money.

"Given that, your current allocation is too aggressive. Your mutual fund's allocation is overexposed to high-risk international and emerging market stocks. The fixed-income percentage is positioned in long-term bonds, creating a higher risk based on the current interest rate environment. When interest rates increase, as they have been doing, long bonds lose value. A sizable adjustment would be necessary to correct this mistake.

"Your combined fees totaled an average of 0.96 percent, which is low for a portfolio of mutual funds, but high when compared with a portfolio of exchange-traded funds. A proper assortment in ETFs would be about 0.15 to 0.30 percent.

"When I performed a Great Recession Period—November 2007 through March 2009—stress test on your combined portfolios, it indicated a loss of 41 percent. That's significantly higher than your risk profile assessment indicated would be acceptable."

After reviewing the reports and much more discussion, everyone sat back and took a deep breath. Mr. Jetton spoke first.

"As you can tell, I like much of what you've been doing. If you continue as you are, with some adjustments, you should be okay. I strongly suggest changing your investment allocations and increasing your savings. You need to address the beneficiary issue sooner rather than later and get direct billing on your IRA so you can deduct the fee.

"I would enjoy the privilege of working for you if you feel we're a good fit. I do."

Lisa and Mark looked at each other and smiled, then Lisa said, "Well, we agree. Mark and I felt this way at our first meeting."

Mark nodded and said, "Yeah—so what's our next step?"

"Excellent, glad you feel that way. I'm going to set up a secure, interactive Life Management Logic web portal for you. This modern-day technology will put you in control by giving you access to all your need-to-know information. Its versatility will help you navigate the financial complexities of life. In short order, you will see its invaluable resourcefulness and ingenuity. This marvelous tool's powerful engine will deliver to you a deep common-sense reasoning ability, which is vital when exploring your planning possibilities. It calculates numerous scenarios to give you examples of how to prepare. You'll be able to see in what manner your life might be different when making small or big changes. It'll put you in the know, and those who know do better than those who don't.

"As I mentioned during your last visit, my L.I.F.E. Formula—Live. Imagine. Focus. Enjoy.® is a comprehensive retirement planning system. It has seven steps. We'll utilize your data input from your Life Management Logic web portal to work through each step.

"Step One in the process is to discover your desires and expectations of what you want new in your life and what will remain the same. Your existence on planet Earth is going to revolve around a different equator. Your life's axis will be tilted in the direction of what can make each day more rewarding, more fulfilling. Your night sky will be jam-packed with brighter, more abundant stars, ones you've never seen. It'll be energizing and exciting.

"You don't want to shy away from the negative, though. Listing your concerns is necessary—these are issues that cause you to think twice, anything that might make you lose sleep. Preparing to meet an adverse outcome head-on may eliminate or improve your result.

"At this point, targeting your retirement life goals will fall into place.

"Step Two requires us to examine two key organizing components and a five-part risk assessment procedure.

We'll inventory all your assets and liabilities and calculate the relationship between them, which will give us an all-important ratio.

"At the same time, we'll examine whether and to what degree your assets are protected from loss. Our lives can be impacted by consequences within our control and beyond our control. Regardless, we must prepare for and be able to limit the damage, even though we hope nothing bad happens.

"You own substantial assets subject to forfeiture if your family were struck by a catastrophic financial event. For most people, a permanent or extended disability would prevent them from collecting their paycheck, which could make paying monthly expenses difficult and has the potential to reduce their savings for retirement, but fortunately for you, income replacement is a company benefit. A health incident perhaps not covered by medical or long-term-care contracts could be an economic disaster.

"Next, I'll check your homeowner and auto policies to see if they are up-to-date and at adequate levels. Part of that would include a review of your liability and umbrella coverage, which provides you with another layer of monetary protection for unintended, careless deeds by you or a family member. If I see any red flags,

I'll prepare a list that you can use to discuss with your insurance agent.

"To make certain all your ducks are in formation we need to confirm whether your estate-planning documents are in order? Yours are not that old, so they should be okay, but I'll review them and give you my non-attorney report, which we'll discuss to see if changes are necessary.

"Another important component of Step Two is a subject no one wants to think about, let alone talk about. Death. However, we'll face this topic head-on. As responsible adults, you must prepare for the unexpected. Statistically, you're going to live a long life, but statistics don't always favor you.

"So the next critical consideration to examine is whether you have enough survivor's resources to provide money if one of you die. If the unexpected were to happen, the survivor would experience incomprehensible emotional and financial devastation. The emotional jolt will heal in time. The financial ruin may never heal. We need to address difficult issues. We'll look at 'what if' examples to give you help on how to plan around these potential disasters.

"Finally, when strategizing to protect your money, one area often overlooked is how to save on income taxes. In some families, taxes are a major outflow of money. Tax planning isn't easy and doesn't always produce positive results; however, if you don't examine this important and complicated subject, you'll never know how much you might've saved. Remember what Ben Franklin said: 'A penny saved is a penny got.' And that penny can be added to your retirement funds.

"Step Three in my system is a tough exercise, but valuable in the long run. Project your expenses in retirement. I'll give you a ledger to make it easier to input the details. This step is difficult, and you might tell me, 'No, I don't want to go there.' Remember, you hire me to give you educated advice. You evaluate my recommendations, then stamp them accepted or refused. It's your choice. If you accept this one, you'll see whether there are any current expenses that you can redirect to savings. The more you save now, the happier you'll be when your paychecks stop. Again, it's up to you. It's a smart move to calculate an accurate number.

"If you agree, the second part is to compute a ratio between expenses and your guaranteed income.

"Step Four is building your personal plan. I'll use my proprietary system refined after years of trial and error. Your information will be engineered into a written document that details your financial life in a visual format. Seeing the lay of the land makes it easier to identify the bumps in the road ahead.

"At that point, it'll be time to fine-tune your vision. We'll measure the first three steps and determine necessary remedies.

"This is when we look at your needs, wants, and possibilities to determine if they're all doable. Do you need to modify any component? Do you need to remove, refine, or want to add other goals? Your preparation will increase the potential to power a positive result.

"We need to study each goal category that has a weakness or deficiency and resolve it as best we can. We may not be able to effectively tackle each one immediately, but we'll create a timetable and factor them into the big picture.

"Next, we'll refine how you feel about risk, and complete an Investment Policy Declaration, or IPD, to guide us in allocating your money properly. The IPD will order a specific formula for investing your assets and our mutual management of your portfolio. Each dollar will be repositioned in low cost investments.

"Step Five is the implementation, or action, step. It's where the rubber meets the road. This step puts you in charge, in control of your future. Nothing happens unless you put your foot on the gas and outrun procrastination. Gearing up together, and accelerating through that miserable monster will enhance your outcome. You'll be able to monitor everything with your Life Management Logic website.

"Step Six is major. Annually, we'll review your L.I.F.E. Formula to determine progress and whether the original assumptions about inflation, income taxes, Social Security, pensions, growth on investments, monthly expenses, and everything else were accurate. Did anything happen during the year that would require making a change like a new development. Is your projected lifestyle unfolding as planned or do you want to change directions? We must monitor progress and continually check your assumptions to see if they're on target.

"None of this effort will work without Step Seven. The hours, brainpower, calculations, projections, soul-searching, thinking, rethinking, and final decisions can't lull you into the misconception that your work is done and that you can rest on your laurels. The truth is, you should never relegate this part of your life to a shelf in the closet—you're never really done. You must use your Life Management Logic web portal to stay in touch with the everyday workings of your financial life. Give it the attention it deserves.

"So again, together we'll review the progress of the first 6 steps annually. They won't work without Step Seven, which is—start over. We must continue to review each step to make certain we're on track. We'll do this once a year."

Lisa was listening intently. She thought of Ace and the value of everything he had taught Mark before the dreams started fading. As she absorbed Chico's words, a new feeling of confidence lifted her spirits higher. She knew that their path to this new life would be less bumpy with Chico by their side.

Lisa said, "I feel good, really good. How often will we get together?"

"That depends on you. We'll start with every three months. Should you decide, after time, that quarterly is too often, we can modify our schedule to every four months or however often would be better suited to your style and pleasure. Our key purpose is to keep you up-to-date, in the know. To be on top of what's happening in your financial life. As you become fully engaged in using your Life Management Logic web portal, you may decide that meeting every three months isn't necessary. It's up to you.

"It's also important you know that we're not stuck

with seeing each other only on some fixed schedule. If an issue develops in your financial life that you want my help to resolve, I'll be there for you."

Lisa asked, "What does that mean?"

"Here's an example. I met with, let's call them Mary and Tom two weeks ago, for their annual review. Afterward, we scheduled our appointment for next year, but Tom called the following Monday to say he wanted to meet ASAP to get my opinion on something very important.

"When we met, Mary said, 'We attended a seminar presented by an attorney on how to qualify for Medi-Cal,' which is California's version of Medicaid.

"After the seminar, they signed up to meet with him at his office. That meeting repeated what he had said at his seminar presentation. They were told they could lose all their assets if they needed to enter a skilled nursing facility. The attorney told them the statistics were high, and they could be risking all their money. Nothing would be left to their children. It captured their attention.

"I looked at the attorney's folder, which was loaded with scary material. It was a sales pitch for why they should preplan qualifying.

"Even though both were in good health, they started

worrying about losing all their money.

"Tom said 'I should have invested in the long-term-care policy you recommended 10 or 11 years ago, but it's too late now. Too expensive.'

"To help us sort through their urgent concern, we scheduled another visit. I invited my attorney, who specializes in elder law, to join us so she could answer the questions that I couldn't.

"She told Mary and Tom that the way to reorganize assets to qualify is complicated. It needs to be done with the direction of a professional. To receive benefits, you must spend down or divest countable assets, and you can have very little income. Certain assets are exempt when calculating whether you qualify under the asset test. Qualified retirement savings like 401(k) plans and IRAs, a home, an auto, personal property, burial plots, certain annuities, and low-cash-value life insurance policies are exempt.

"After talking further with Mary and Tom, we discovered that when they met with the seminar attorney for their interview, he didn't ask them for a list of assets. If he had, he would've learned their excluded assets totaled a sizable amount, but their countable or nonexcludable assets totaled only $13,453. At that point, it became obvious they didn't need to preplan for this possible event.

"The attorney's pitch wasn't predicated on helping them protect their money. It was designed to get some of their money. He wanted $7,500, whether they were at risk or not. It's an example of why you must be on your toes.

"This is just one reason you might want to get together before a regularly scheduled visit. Anything in your financial life that is causing you concern would be a reason to meet."

Lisa said, "You mentioned long-term care. Recently, I reviewed Mark's benefits package. Convalescent nursing home care was listed. Is it the same thing?"

"Well, convalescent care is different from skilled nursing care. But the attorney was sort of right about what he preached. It's true that a high percentage of older people have health issues that require care, but the majority need only convalescent care, not skilled nursing care.

"Be assured—examining whether your asset protection planning process has any soft spots is part of my L.I.F.E. Formula system."

Lisa felt as though a weight had been lifted from her shoulders. Even though Ace had faded from Mark's dreams, he had given Mark countless ideas about preparing for retirement. After all the dreams, discussions, and consternation, they finally took the initiative and found someone who would take over for Ace and help them get their dollar ducks in a row. A human.

The Nitty-Gritty

You made it. Congratulations! How do you feel? Like a million dollars? You should. You have learned a lot.

But what you have learned is of little importance. It is what you do with what you have learned that measures your worth.

In the **STOP! Read This First** section, I said you need to actively participate with your CFP® in the process of designing your retirement plan. Now you have the knowledge to do your part.

Good luck to you. On second thought, find a qualified CFP® and make your own luck.

Dream Big! Save Big! Live Big!
Happy Retirement!

L.I.F.E. Formula
Live. Imagine. Focus. Enjoy.®

A Comprehensive 7-STEP Retirement Planning System

1) Discovery
   a) Needs
   b) Wants
   c) Expectations
   d) Concerns
   e) Goals

2) Protect Your Assets
   a) Inventory
      i) Assets vs. Liabilities
      ii) Ratio
   b) Five-Part Risk Assessment
      i) Health
      ii) Casualty
      iii) Estate Documents
      iv) Survivor's Resources
      v) Income Tax Exposure

3) Guaranteed Income vs. Disbursements
   a) Ratio of Guaranteed Income to Fixed Expenses
   b) Ratio of Balance of Guaranteed Income to Discretionary Expenses

4) Build Your Plan
- a) Proprietary Planning
  - i) Measure Steps 1, 2, and 3
  - ii) Construct Remedies
- b) Determine Investment Risk Level
- c) Create Investment Policy Declaration (IPD)

5) Take Action
- a) Activate Remedies
- b) Monitor – Life Management Logic

6) Annual Review
- a) Assess Progress – Verify Assumptions
  - i) Inflation
  - ii) Income Tax
  - iii) Expense
  - iv) Growth Rate
  - v) Social Security
  - vi) Pension
  - vii) Investments
  - viii) New Development

7) Start Over
- a) Review First Six Steps Annually — Stay Focused

Financial Principles Simplified

www.ingramcontent.com/pod-product-compliance
Lightning Source LLC
Chambersburg PA
CBHW060546200326
41521CB00007B/499